- PRACTICAL PRINCIPLES -

PUBLISHED by Mike LaBahn & Associates
CONTRIBUTING EDITS by Jenny Pedersen
SPECIAL THANKS to Michael Wourms & Wesley Fulkerson
BOOK DESIGN by Troy Hollinger

4616 Calavo Drive
La Mesa, CA 91941

mikelabahn.com

ISBN 978-0-9910043-4-8
All Rights Reserved. All scriptures are from the New American Standard version of the Bible unless otherwise stated. Mike LaBahn © 2025 All Rights Reserved.

TO MY
WIFE
CHILDREN
GRAND CHILDREN
GREAT GRAND CHILDREN
GREAT GREAT GRAND CHILDREN

FOREWORD - **Robin Hadfield**

It was 1981. Mike and Julie arrived home after another day in the hot, Southern California sun. Two lawn mowers, rakes and other landscaping tools filled the back of their old Ford pickup truck. What began as a Ma and Pa business morphed into a very successful landscaping company, which now employs approximately 250 workers.

Between then and now, Mike burrowed into the study of financial principles from a Biblical perspective, he learned, then applied as he began his life journey as a businessman in the landscaping industry. This book is that life journey; it is the work of a lifetime, his lifetime.

It is my pleasure to write this forward. Mike has lived this book as long as I have known him – some 40 years. He speaks with integrity and thoroughness. You will be enriched as you read.

Table of Contents / **Guide to Book**

	INTRODUCTION	**13**
Chapter 1 -	**PRODUCE WEALTH** 5 PROVERB PRINCIPLES	**19**
Chapter 2 -	**PRODUCE A LEGACY** 5 SCRIPTURAL PRINCIPLES	**33**
Chapter 3 -	**HOW TO BECOME WISE**	**47**
Chapter 4 -	**MORE THAN MONEY** TO BE TRULY RICH	**69**
Chapter 5 -	**EMPOWERING DISCIPLINE**	**87**
Chapter 6 -	**GIVING** YOUR WAY TO RICHES	**97**
Chapter 7 -	**WORKPLACE PROSPERITY** 10 VITAL INSTRUCTIONS	**115**
Chapter 8 -	**FOOLS, FOLLY & FRIVOLITY**	**129**
Chapter 9 -	**LIVING A BETTER LIFE** GOD'S GUIDELINES	**147**
Chapter 10 -	**THE FIRST & LAST WORD**	**169**

PROVERBS

PROVERB'S PRACTICAL PRINCIPLES

MIKE La BAHN

This succinct little book shares some of the basic, yet universal truths in the Book of Proverbs that are vital guidelines for living in today's challenging and often confusing world. Just as they were crucial guidelines for living when they were written by Solomon and other authors (such as Agur and King Lemuel), centuries ago, so too they are crucial guidelines now and forever vital to your personal life, to your business, and to your family's success – until the end of time!

Proverbs is a philosophical book that seeks to answer the eternal question: "How should we live our lives?" The Book of Proverbs contains what I call "maxims" short, easy-to-remember expressions of basic biblical guidelines, principles for living, general truths, or rules of conduct. They might be described as "nuggets of wisdom."

The maxims in Proverbs express general principles of how God runs the world. This is an extremely important point, since general principles are not the same as the infallible promises or the commandments of God. Proverbs should not be taken as absolute, unconditional covenants from God, but rather as generalizations that can improve your life; and these generalizations can have exceptions. For example, "those who live wisely" are generally blessed with success in parenting, in finances, and with a long life. The fool, on the other hand, can generally expect trouble in this life with his children and his finances because of his defiance of God's principles of wisdom.

The exceptions to these maxims never nullify the wisdom of these sayings! Proverbs will make great reading and provide worthwhile wisdom if you do not read it as a book of absolute promises or rigid rules concerning living. It is not very difficult in our daily lives to discern the exceptions to the generalities in Proverbs. For instance, Proverbs 28:19 declares: *He who tills his* land will have plenty of food, but he who follows empty pursuits will have poverty in plenty.*

Of course, this generally is the case. Hard work normally produces income. However, there are many industrious farmers who diligently work their land extremely hard, yet they can go hungry and even bankrupt in times of a severe drought or a freeze; both weather conditions (which the farmer cannot control) have the potential to ruin their crops. Tremper Longman, author of *How to Read Proverbs*, clarifies this principle by stating that these sayings "are true if all things are equal."[1] These maxims do not intend to take account of all the possibilities. A storm or a drought can undermine even the hardest efforts, but if one does not perform the proper labor, then there is no chance for a good crop.

On the other hand, unfortunately, through the years we have seen instances of an unemployed loafer plop down $1 on a lottery ticket and then win millions in an instant drawing. In many of these cases (where wealth is obtained without work), the loafer fails to alter his lazy habits, and spends his new-found fortune like a fool, often becoming broke again in a matter of a few years.

Maxims are general guidelines, and there will always be exceptions! The Book of Proverbs simply tells us how life works most of the time and over time! (We can worry about the exceptions after we master the general rules.) If you try and live by the exceptions, your life will end up a disaster. But, if you follow these general rules – living a godly, moral, hard-working and wise life – you will likely reap wonderful rewards over your lifetime.

Proverbial teaching is one of the most ancient methods of instruction. It was well suited to the time when books were scarce and philosophy was little understood. The mind, not used to the slow process of reasoning, was more easily engaged by terse sentences that

---

[1] - Longman III, Tremper, "Proverbs," 2007, pages 85, 134, 240, 277; Grand Rapids, MI, Baker Academic.

expressed a striking thought in a few words. The writer of Proverbs himself has perhaps given the best definition of these maxims when he wrote in Proverbs 25:11,

Like apples of gold in settings of silver is a word spoken in right circumstances.

Professor Grant Osborne, a noted expert on the principles of interpreting Scripture, writes that by their very nature, (the Proverbs) are statements intended "to give advice rather than to establish codes by which God works." Renowned Bible teacher Chuck Swindoll characterizes the Book of Proverbs as "the most practical book in the Old Testament, and, in many ways, the most practical book in all the Bible."[2]

The distinctive characteristic of the Book of Proverbs is that it is a book for the young. The answer to the question, "How can a young man keep his way pure?" is fully answered in the Book of Proverbs. Proverbs specifically states that it was written so that young people could learn from it (Proverbs 1:4; 4:1).

The individual scriptures I have chosen to share here are my personal favorites; a choice selection of biblical principles from Proverbs from the observations of Mike LaBahn.

I hope these principles bless you and help you keep your life on course in the midst of the many challenges of running a business, your personal life, or a family. Please know that I learned to apply most of these principles from hard experience. My commercial landscape company, LaBahn's Landscaping, was built from the bottom up on these biblical principles. We have grown from a one-man operation to employing 250 workers not because I am a brilliant businessman, but because I have read and applied the biblical lessons from Proverbs and other places in Scripture.

---

2 - Swindoll, Charles, "The Living Insights Study Bible," 1996, Zondervan, Nashville, TN, 37201

My prayer is that these principles will convict you and help you prosper in whatever objectives you have in your life.

– Mike LaBahn

Chapter 1

PRODUCE WEALTH
5 PROVERB PRINCIPLES

What vital biblical virtues should be employed in your business if you want to prosper God's way?

What does "wealth without wisdom" mean to you?

Would your employer describe you as a diligent worker? If so, why or why not?

Give biblical reasons why integrity is important in the workplace and in your own life.

Describe a specific situation where it might be important to 'hold your tongue' in the workplace.

What are the biblical characteristics of a sluggard?

Does hard work still matter?

In the wacky world we live in (as of January, 2014), there were over 1,426 billionaires worldwide, with a combined net worth of $5.4 trillion. Millionaires seem to live on virtually every block in the United States. The old concept of an honest, hard day's work seems to mean less and less to the younger generation; as evidence of "quick wealth" they point to ample evidence of men and women in their twenties who have become millionaires (and even billionaires) quickly through internet and communications commerce.

Because of this "get rich quick" mentality, in my landscaping business I find it harder and harder to locate and hire conscientious young workers who are willing to put in an honest day's work in return for a fair wage. I believe that too many of our younger generation are dramatically influenced by the entertainers, internet entrepreneurs, lottery winners, and popular sports figures who receive multi-million dollar incomes in very short periods of time. After all, these young tycoons are living proof that there is an easy way to experience huge riches and enjoy a self-serving lifestyle.

Let's face it – we live in a world of instant millionaires, even billionaires, from IPO's (Initial Public Offerings in the stock market) and from celebrities in the entertainment and sports industries. Young men and women just out of college are signing multi-year, million dollar sports contracts, entertainers barely old enough to drive a car are buying ten million dollar mansions and driving two seated, speedy sports cars that cost two hundred thousand dollars. Internet founders have dropped out of college to start companies worth billions within a decade. Lottery winners have gone from the slums to Beverly Hills with a winning ticket.

When the average young worker reads about this huge influx of wealth to other young people who are making large amounts of money in a short time, it impacts and changes the American dream – perhaps forever. No longer is the work ethic motto, "Work hard for thirty years, pay off your home and your debts, and then retire." Instead, the new mantra that our youth hear virtually every single day is, "Work hard for a few years in sports, in entertainment, or in developing a business to go public or be sold, then live like a king the rest of your life."

WHAT DOES THE BIBLE SAY?

I believe the real question we must ask to discern a biblical perspective on work and wealth is, "What Scriptural principles produce real, sustaining wealth?" Youth today are asking, "Does God still value and reward honest, hard work?" To answer these two probing questions, this chapter shares five Scriptural principles related to work; these principles will produce wealth – according to God's Word.

Many do not realize that there is a biblical prescription on how to become rich, and it is clearly and precisely described in God's Word (especially in Proverbs). As you study these biblical principles for wealth, I believe you will discover that there is nothing in God's Word that indicates His way to wealth is for you to work for a few years, hit it big, and then retire. Or, to plan to make a lifetime's worth of income through a lottery ticket.

1 - EXERCISE PERSONAL AND BUSINESS DILIGENCE

Poor is he who works with a negligent hand, but the hand of the diligent makes rich. Proverbs 10:4

A key biblical element in the process of becoming "rich" is what we know today as "due diligence". A diligent person is one who is industrious, meticulous, conscientious, thorough, attentive to his task, and employs a careful approach to whatever assignment he performs.

Conversely, a "negligent hand" will likely produce poverty in your life. The negligent person is the exact opposite of the diligent worker; he or she is careless, inattentive, slipshod, lax, slack, and far too casual about the assignment at hand.

The biblical message here is clear: negligence tends to make you poor, and proper diligence will ultimately tend to bring wealth into your life. This is not an isolated message, limited to one Scripture; this message is diligently conveyed in other parts of God's Word as well (Proverbs 4:23; 12:27; Romans 12:8; 12:11; Hebrews 6:11; 2 Peter 1:5). Another Scripture in Proverbs states:

The soul of the sluggard craves and gets nothing, but the soul of the diligent is made fat. Proverbs 13:4

What is a sluggard? Well, "sluggard" isn't a word we commonly use to describe people today, nor is it one easily found in a normal dictionary, but believe me, you have met many a sluggard in your life. Charles Bridges says that "...the sluggard craves the fruit of diligence without the diligence that produces it."³

A partial portrait of a sluggard is described in Proverbs 26:13-16:

The sluggard says, "There is a lion in the road! A lion is in the open square!" As the door turns on its hinges, so does the sluggard on his bed. The sluggard buries his hand in the dish; he is weary of bringing it to his mouth again. The sluggard is wiser in his own eyes than seven men who can give a discreet answer.

Tremper Longman, a reputed Old Testament scholar, states that "...the cravings of the lazy go unrequited, presumably because they are unwilling to work toward their goals."⁴

The sluggard in the workplace manifests four undesirable character flaws:

1. He makes every excuse, no matter how outlandish, to stay at home and not go to work (verse 13).
2. His main "activity" of choice is turning in his bed (verse 14).
3. He is so lazy that he is even reluctant to do those things that will benefit him directly (verse 15).
4. He mistakenly believes that his ability to shun work is the mark of true wisdom (verse 16).

A sluggard is that person you hire to mow and rake your backyard, but he takes twice as long as he should to do it, charges twice as much, and does only half of what you have asked him to do. A sluggard is that lady in your office who takes thirty minute breaks at the water cooler to visit with other clerks in the office, makes sure her make-up and hair are always just right by visiting the women's lounge repeatedly throughout

---

3 - Longman III, Tremper, "Proverbs," 2007, pgs 284; Grand Rapids, MI, Baker Academic.
4 - Bridges, Charles, "Proverbs" 2001, Pg 94; Wheaton, IL 60187, Good News Publishers

the day, and usually fails to meet even the minimum work expectations assigned to her for the day. Neither "sluggard" is likely to receive a promotion anytime soon; in fact, termination slips are probably in their futures.

Parallel to the sluggard is the busybody, as portrayed in Proverbs 26:17-22:

Like one who takes a dog by the ears is he who passes by and meddles with strife not belonging to him. Like a madman who throws firebrands, arrows and death, so is the man who deceives his neighbor, and says, "Was I not joking?" For lack of wood the fire goes out, and where there is no whisperer, contention quiets down. Like charcoal to hot embers and wood to fire, so is a contentious man to kindle strife. The words of a whisperer are like dainty morsels, and they go down into the innermost parts of the body.

The busybody worker meddles in the quarrels of others and spreads rumors in the office. The busybody will lie or add rumors to a dispute to keep it going, fueling the fire of others. The busybody absolutely loves gossip, and stirring up trouble with fellow workers.

Promotion will normally go to the "diligent" worker in the backyard who does more than expected in less amount of time, for less money; promotion will likely go to the clerk who types faster and more accurately, with no distractions, than others in the office.

Poor is he who works with a negligent hand, but the hand of the diligent makes rich. Proverbs 10:4

This is not only "common sense," it is biblical sense. This principle of diligence is also emphasized in Proverbs 21:5.

The plans of the diligent lead surely to advantage, but

everyone who is hasty comes surely to poverty.

When a person diligently applies himself, it will lead to "advantage." Proverbs 10:5 declares, *"He who gathers in summer is a son who acts wisely, but he who sleeps in harvest is a son who acts shamefully."* What businessman or woman would not want to "act wisely" and have an advantage over the competition? Well, believe it or not, from my experience in the landscape business, and from the myriad of experiences of my friends in other types of businesses, simply being diligent to do those things you promise to do does indeed give you an advantage over your competition!

Of course, the opposite of operating with diligence is operating in haste: doing or saying things without sufficient consideration of their consequences. Haste is worse than foolishness.

Do you see a man who speaks in haste? There is more hope for a fool than for him. Proverbs 29:20

When a business operates too quickly, without sufficient consideration to the consequences of doing a job too quickly, it too is worse than foolishness. Doing the work too quickly can lead to poor results and amount to a deviation from God's path of diligence. Hasty decision making and hasty performance in the workplace should be avoided whenever possible.

For reasons I could never grasp (and still cannot), there are "businessmen" out in the working force who are trying to produce wealth from their business but are not even diligent enough to show up when they promise, to complete jobs on time, or return phone calls when they say they will.

However, if you do your job carelessly and quickly–being too hasty–it will result in "call backs" and complaints to fix what should have been done right the first time. These call backs cost a businessman money, and most importantly, hurt your reputation, thus cutting down on the likelihood of any future referrals. Being too hasty will "surely lead to poverty."

In summary, do the basic biblical principles the competition is not doing – that simple advantage will lead to wealth!

2 - WORK WHEN THERE IS A NEED

Far too many businessmen fail to seize the opportunity at hand to be productive when the jobs are available and abundant in their particular field. Instead of putting on extra men to meet the demand, they walk in fear, keeping their crews small, failing to harvest the full crop that is available in their workplace. To me, that would be like a farmer planting three acres of tomatoes, and after he has harvested one, walks away from the other two acres, reasoning: "I've got all I need for now." Proverbs 10:5 warns against such laxness:

He who gathers in summer is a son who acts wisely, but he who sleeps in harvest is a son who acts shamefully.

No business boom and no harvest of crops lasts forever. If construction is booming in your city, the Bible advises that you act wisely and gather in the jobs as they present themselves to you as a harvest. If you instead decide not to expand to bring in that business harvest, you are likely to see an unwanted result – your business will remain stagnant and stale while others around you are becoming rich.

The old adage, "Make hay when the sun shines" is not just a motto; it is a saying that has evolved from the principles in God's Word. Do not go golfing when there is a harvest to be picked; do not go fishing when the tomatoes are ripe for picking.

3 - LIVE A RIGHTEOUS LIFE

To prosper in business, or to be promoted in the workplace, it is imperative that you maintain a righteous life, practice integrity, obey God's commandments, and adhere to biblical principles in every area of your life. While this is a solid biblical principle, it should be noted here that this is not an all-encompassing formula for wealth; there are many instances in the Bible where men and women who lived righteous lives did not receive wealth. The most obvious is Jesus, who never owned a home, ran a business empire, or earned copious amounts of money.

But, the wisdom in Proverbs does make it clear that if you cheat your clients, or steal from your boss, or lie to those in your workplace, your reputation will decline, and you will not enjoy favor with your workers, your boss, or your clients.

The memory of the righteous is blessed, but the name of the wicked will rot. Proverbs 10:7

Proverbs is a philosophical and a theological book that seeks to answer that eternal question we all ask, "How should we live our lives?" In Proverbs, we learn that as we live good and honest lives, we will be blessed; but, if we lie, cheat and deceive, our wicked lives will produce a rotten stench repulsive to all.

For he will never be shaken; the righteous will be remembered forever. Psalm 112:6

"Forever" is a long time. This verse clearly explains that when you live a righteous life, in essence, you will establish a legacy, a memorial, for your children and your children's children that will be remembered and honored long after you become fodder for a worm farm.

You have rebuked the nations, You have destroyed the wicked; You have blotted out their name forever and ever. Psalm 9:5

This is the second promise involving "forever" – and it represents an unwanted but all-too-warranted legacy. When your work ethic reflects deception and lying, when your life goes against the Scriptural mandates of God's Word, then you will cast a blot upon your family name that will be passed on to your children and future generations. If you fail to live a righteous life, Psalm 109:13 warns, *"Let his posterity be cut off; in a following generation let their name be blotted out."*

In essence, there are eternal rewards for those who perform with righteous ethics in the workplace and eternal disgrace for those who fail to live in accordance with God's laws. Ecclesiastes 8:10 makes this curse for unrighteous living abundantly clear:

So then, I have seen the wicked buried, those who used to go in and out from the holy place, and they are soon forgotten in the city where they did thus. This too is futility.

4 - MIND YOUR OWN BUSINES!

He who tills his land will have plenty of bread, but he who pursues worthless things lacks sense. Proverbs 12:11

God gives each of us land to till (to condition or plow the soil) – that "land" is our business. For some, the land you till will be the responsibility you receive from your boss at work. For others, it is the clients God brings to you as an independent businessperson. Whatever your case, your responsibility is the same: to properly till your land so that you will have food on the table.

If you ignore the responsibility you have for the land God has given you to till, instead choosing to play games on a computer at work, texting, emailing, calling up friends, or going golfing when there are pressing matters at work to be addressed, or indulge in time-consuming, meaningless conversations ("worthless things"), you essentially become a fool chasing the whims, fancies and empty pursuits of others. (How many of us live vicariously through the latest exploits of an entertainer or a sports hero, wasting countless hours of time watching sporting events, instead of tilling our land?)
Proverbs 28:19:

He who tills his land will have plenty of food, but he who follows empty pursuits will have poverty in plenty.

As you diligently work your land, you will end up with plenty of food. But, if you decide to simply play and party, your reward will be an empty plate.

5 - DO NOT REVEAL ALL YOU KNOW

A prudent man conceals knowledge, but the heart of fools proclaims folly. Proverbs 12:23

I find this principle particularly important yet seldom practiced. All too often successful business people have a tendency to demonstrate too quickly what they know. This biblical principle suggests that prudent people are selective in how, where and when they share their knowledge. A prudent man does not always need to prove he is right in front of others, nor does he need to prove others wrong. It is only the fool who has no filter from his brain to his mouth and simply spouts out what he knows in every situation without any consideration for the eventual cost. It has been said that "It is better to be thought a fool than to open your mouth and remove all doubt." A wise man never flaunts knowledge! Talkative fools broadcast their every thought, radiating silliness.

Wise men store up knowledge, but with the mouth of the foolish, ruin is at hand. Proverbs 10:14

To "store up" knowledge means to keep that information in storage to be used for the proper occasion.
These Scriptures bring up another interesting issue. Control over gossip in the office and the ability to keep work secrets and important proprietary information within a company are vital to any company's success. Failure to do so can sabotage a company and destroy the trust so desperately needed between the employees working for that company and upper management. To conduct business in the world today, an office needs prudent men and women, not fools.

Every prudent man acts with knowledge, but a fool displays folly. Proverbs 13:16

There are numerous admonitions in God's Word concerning how important it is to hold our tongue in various situations.

He who goes about as a talebearer reveals secrets, but he who is trustworthy conceals a matter. Proverbs 11:13

The ability to "conceal" a matter implies that the person with the information can be trusted to keep it to themselves when it is vital to do so.

The tongue of the wise makes knowledge acceptable, but the mouth of fools spouts folly. Proverbs 15:2

Fools clearly do not have verbal filters, but act as a non-stop faucet that spouts continually without an off or on handle.

These scriptures are shared for your reference, your knowledge, and hopefully, to further your conviction that our thoughts and what comes out of our mouth should be filtered.

WEALTH WITHOUT WISDOM

While no one can deny that instant wealth does occur, it is clearly not the biblical pattern, nor is it the way that produces character, wisdom, and leadership qualities for most people. We all have read the tragic stories of the instant lotto millionaires who have, within a few years, squandered all of their "quick" money and become broke again, all too often finding their lives ravaged by undisciplined living, unchecked excesses, and foolish decisions.

Proverbs reveals how we can best be productive in the workplace, receive the hard-earned wealth we desire to bless our families, and ultimately, to bless the Kingdom of God.

Chapter 2

PRODUCE A LEGACY
5 SCRIPTURAL PRINCIPLES

What reputation do you think you have in your business? What biblical principles can you employ to improve that reputation?

To leave a legacy for your family, what traits do you need to practice now?

Do you honestly weigh the ideas and corrections of others, or just listen politely and then ignore them? If you discount them, what does Proverbs say about your future?

Why does the Bible say that a Christian should not charge interest?

What do you need to change most about the condition of your life today?

...your children's children.

1 - DILIGENCE PRODUCES A LEGACY OF DOMINANCE, RULE, AUTHORITY AND PROMOTION

The hand of the diligent will rule, but the slack hand (laziness) *will be put to forced labor.* Proverbs 12:24

The diligent workers find freedom in their work and will be given more and more authority through earned trust, eventually leading to promotion and authority over others. The diligent worker is the one the boss can trust, and that is the person who will likely be singled out for promotion and increased authority. Those who fail to exercise their assigned responsibilities will normally be demoted to the level where they will be given jobs that require little or no diligence; they will be given assignments where a boss will supervise their every move. Those who are lazy will be oppressed by their work.

I can hear many a businessman reading this book thinking, "Mike, tell it like it is. That is the absolute truth." Unfortunately, businessmen often fail to realize that these same Scriptures apply to them as well.

Businessmen and women, if you are diligent in the workplace, you will attract clients who appreciate you and will want to stay with your company, basically giving you authority over their "land". You will "rule" in your chosen area of expertise and produce a virtual legacy (and great reputation) in your business. But, if you fail to do what you say you are going to do, you just might wake up one morning only to discover that your business no longer exists, and a competitor is now dominant in your industry. Be diligent so that forced labor will not be your fate.

Their descendants who were left after them in the land whom the sons of Israel were unable to destroy utterly, from them Solomon levied forced laborers, even to this day. I Kings 9:21

If you want to receive promotion, authority and dominance in your workplace, then laziness cannot be a part of your lifestyle.

A lazy man does not roast his prey, but the precious possession of a man is diligence. Proverbs 12:17

In your list of precious, valuable qualities and personal possessions, would "diligence" be in your top 10? God's Word describes diligence as "a precious possession"; the life of a lazy man does not even produce enough food for a simple family BBQ. A lazy life is an empty life, without authority or the ability to rule. But, the man who is disciplined and has the diligence to get up every morning and report to work on time – that's the person who gets the job done and receives the biblical blessings, creating a living legacy.

Remember that "sluggard" I wrote about earlier? Well, he ultimately becomes so lazy that he cannot even lift his fork to feed himself!

The sluggard buries his hand in the dish, but will not even bring it back to his mouth. Proverbs 19:24

Can you imagine becoming so lazy that you

would stick your fork into a slice of luscious apple pie, but then become too lazy to raise that fork to your mouth? Proverbs 26:15 says that is the fate of the sluggard!

The sluggard buries his hand in the dish; he is weary of bringing it to his mouth again. Now that is one lazy fellow, and he will receive "nothing" such as a promotion or a position of dominance, since he is not putting out anything.

The soul of the sluggard craves and gets nothing, but the soul of the diligent is made fat. Proverbs 13:4

Do you see a continuing theme here? A person of indolence (sluggard; laziness) wants it all, but receives and earns nothing, and leaves no legacy. It is the energetic, diligent person who shows up on time for work, and leads a productive life, who becomes rich in the things of this earth, and receives the authority and rule over others!

Poverty and shame will come to him who neglects discipline, but he who regards reproof will be honored. Proverbs 13:18

The question is basic: Do you want poverty and shame in your future or riches and a living legacy? To welcome reproof and let it change our ways is a mark of maturity that most people will admire. The proper response to correction can make us more effective and our businesses more profitable. To disdain correction, in contrast, leaves us to our own resources, severs us from the wisdom of others, diminishes our respect with our associates, and could well lead to poverty and shame.

If you want riches and a family legacy, then decide to have discipline in your life; it is really that simple. I personally believe that discipline is one of the most important character traits that a person can develop, but it is also (from my personal observation of others through the decades) one of the most difficult to master. We are living in a "go for it" generation, and discipline is the one character trait this generation simply seems to refuse to apply in their lives. It is too old fashioned. It is far easier to finance a new car than to exercise the discipline of saving for five years (and driving an older car) so you can pay cash for the new car. It is more convenient to refinance your house, robbing yourself of hard-earned equity, so you can spend foolish "easy" money on needless dinners and vacations you cannot normally afford, ultimately ending up deeply in debt or homeless.

But, he who receives reproof (discipline) will be honored! Of course, **to truly receive correction requires the humility to listen.**

When I saw, I reflected upon it; I looked, and received instruction. Proverbs 24:32

It is important that, when others are courageous enough to give input, we take a long look at what they are saying to us, giving it legitimate reflection (instead of just brushing off their words). Then, after reflection, you decide to put their words into action if what they say rings true in your life. Remember that sluggard? He just keeps popping up in Scripture, and here he is again.

The sluggard is wiser in his own eyes than seven men who can give a discreet answer. Proverbs 26:16

Dreamers fantasize their own self-importance, and some deceive themselves into believing that they are smarter than all the business textbooks combined! But look at what God's Word considers as a wise man:

Be wise, my son, and make my heart glad, that I may

reply to him who reproaches me. Proverbs 27:11

He who embraces correction will live an honored, productive life! That is why it is important for a wise son to be a credit to his father and to aid him in difficulty with appropriate encouragement. This may be true in reverse order as well.

Friend, do not be a fool and live an undisciplined life. *A fool rejects his father's discipline (and the discipline of those in authority over him), but he who regards reproof is sensible.* Proverbs 15:5

On the other hand, *He who neglects discipline despises himself, but he who listens to reproof acquires understanding.* Proverbs 15:32

2 - LEAVE AN INHERITANCE AND A LEGACY

A good man leaves an inheritance to his children's children, and the wealth of the sinner is stored up for the righteous. Proverbs 13:22

Entire books have been written on this biblical principle. God's Word declares that a good life gets passed on to the children and grandchildren, and ill-gotten wealth ends up with good people. In the above Scripture, the verb structure of "leaves an inheritance" does not mean that the "good man" will take his inheritance away from his sons and give it to others. In fact, that would be a great curse to his family. Instead, this Scripture simply means that a good man will transmit his riches to all of his posterity—his children, and his children's children (at least for two generations). Clearly, God's Word encourages us to leave an inheritance to our family.

You may have heard about a movement called

"The Giving Pledge" formed by Bill and Melinda Gates and Warren Buffet. The Giving Pledge encourages fellow billionaires to give away at least fifty percent of their wealth to philanthropic causes for the betterment of our world (at the time of this writing, 122 billionaires from 12 different countries have agreed to this pledge). In these cases of extreme wealth, these men and women are not ignoring the biblical principle of leaving money to their children, but are simply recognizing that they have enough money to help others, and to still leave a solid financial foundation for their future descendants.

Whatever your financial situation, start planning today for ways you can bless not only your children through an inheritance, but your children's children. However, let me caution that this should NOT be taken as a universal statement. Many a good man has no inheritance to leave, and some have no children who survive them, let alone have "children's children." The intent here of Proverbs 13:22 is that a good man's estate remain with his family, while the wealth of the wicked does not. In the divine providence of God, all wealth ultimately will belong to the righteous.

In my book, *Money Management God's Way*, I share how, for just a small amount set aside each month, you can start investment funds for your children and grandchildren that, through compound interest, will ultimately make them millionaires! By saying "his children's children," the Word means that at least two generations will be beneficiaries of a good man.

He who increases his wealth by interest and usury gathers it for him who is gracious to the poor. Proverbs 28:8

I believe this truth is founded in another Scriptural truth that declares, "What you sow you will reap."

SHOULD A CHRISTIAN CHARGE INTEREST?

The Bible teaches, as a general rule, that Christians are to help persons who are in real need and to refrain from charging interest in such situations. We are challenged to love our neighbor and not take advantage of his financial difficulties. Jesus declared, *"Give to him who asks you, and from him who wants to borrow from you do not turn away."* Matthew 5:42

The Old Testament equivalent of this principle occurs in Leviticus 25:35-38:

If one of your brethren becomes poor, and falls into poverty among you, then you shall help him, like a stranger or a sojourner, that he may live with you. Take no usury or interest from him; but fear your God, that your brother may live with you. You shall not lend him your money for usury, nor lend him your food at a profit. I am the LORD your God, who brought you out of the land of Egypt, to give you the land of Canaan and to be your God.

The general principle that arises from these Scriptures is that we should not exploit the poor in his distress. Solomon wrote:

Do not rob the poor because he is poor, nor oppress the afflicted at the gate; for the LORD will plead their cause, and plunder the soul of those who plunder them. Proverbs 22:22-23

By charging interest, we are in effect deepening the borrower's debt, thus making him weaker and poorer in the process. I believe we need to follow the Golden Rule, and consider how we would feel were the situation reversed.

The exception: although a Christian's attitude should be one of giving, sharing, and helping in meeting

---

Golden Rule - Do unto others as you would have them do unto you.
Matthew 7:12

the needs of the less fortunate, there are instances when I believe it is permissible to accept interest. For example, if money is loaned to another individual purely as a business proposition so that person can make more money, then it is not wrong to collect a reasonable amount of interest so that both parties are sharing in the profits. It is also proper to accept interest from money placed in savings accounts, or in bonds, since the money is earning the increase. That interest is in no way hurting anyone else.

However, if you sow ill-gotten gains into your inheritance by charging usury (excessive interest) to others, the reaping of ill-gotten returns will ultimately be your fatal harvest. The Old Testament Law forbade the charging of interest to fellow Jews.

You shall not charge interest to your countrymen: interest on money, food, or anything that may be loaned at interest. You may charge interest to a foreigner, but to your countrymen you shall not charge interest, so that the Lord your God may bless you in all that you undertake in the land which you are about to enter to possess. Deuteronomy 23:19-20

However, that mandate was unfortunately often violated (Nehemiah 5:7,11; Ezekiel 22:12), and generally this resulted in the wealth being forfeited to someone else who treats the poor fairly..."*the wealth of the sinner is laid up for the just.*" (Also see Proverbs 14:31)

Though he piles up silver like dust and prepares garments as plentiful as the clay, he may prepare it, but the just will wear it and the innocent will divide the silver. Job 27:16-17

One of my very favorite Scriptures reinforces this area of sowing good seeds in your financial life for them to be a sustaining legacy to future generations:

I have been young and now I am old, yet I have not seen the righteous forsaken or his descendants begging bread. Psalm 37:25

What parent would not want to leave that kind of inheritance for their children, and their children's children?

3 - ACTION PLAN REQUIRED, NOT JUST IDEAS

In all labor there is profit, but mere talk leads only to poverty. Proverbs 14:23

Hard work always pays off. When you have an idea, and you believe in it, convert it into action through hard work!

Everyone reading this book knows someone I call "the great idea man." Every time you meet him he's got a new scheme, a new idea for making money.

"We will find every isolated little mountain town in the country and bring those tiny towns the internet through satellite technology and relay towers. These little towns are ignored by the big internet providers. My plan will make us all rich. All I need is for somebody to give me $1,500,000 to help launch the start up."

The next week when you meet "the great idea man" he is now talking about copper futures. Two months later he is on to investing in raw land which he plans to convert into a megaresort – with the help of a few solid investors who can put up the $100 million it will take to make his great ideas happen.

Friend, ideas without implementation are simply hot air and will not produce a legacy in this lifetime. Ideas by themselves will not feed your family or help your reputation. Some people just talk, but they do not act. People can almost be classified into two areas: talking people or people of action.

Most successful businesses took years for the initial idea and plans to properly evolve. I first started my landscaping business with a lawnmower; my initial vision was to earn enough income to feed my family and pay our monthly bills. Today, I employ over 100 people, and my original idea of how I was going to earn my income has changed drastically.

With each new idea, I had to put in labor, sweat, discipline and muscle to change or amplify the plan and direction of the company. Today, we are commercial landscapers, and it has been quite a while since I've pushed a lawnmower to put food on the table. In those early years, my motivation was best described by Proverbs 16:26:

A worker's appetite works for him, for his hunger urges him on.

Self-interest is the great, universal motivator. Those days of wondering when the next check was coming in, those days of chasing the mailman, provided my "appetite" to work to build a legacy for my immediate family and my children's children.

Laziness casts into a deep sleep, and an idle man will suffer hunger. Proverbs 19:15

As silly and as obvious as it may sound, it still remains a Scriptural truth that life collapses on loafers; those who are lazy will go hungry. According to Tremper Longman, Proverbs parodies laziness more than any other type of foolishness.[5] Laziness is the height of foolish behavior, and deserves to be parodied. After all, it leads to difficult consequences for both the individual and the community, and it is easily remedied.

I should note here an important truth powerfully expressed in the book *An Introduction to the Poetic Books of the Bible* by C. Hassell Bullock. He shared that the Proverbs are "not legal guarantees from God," but instead are "guidelines for good behavior."[6] Hopefully, that important theme is being properly conveyed and reinforced as I share these biblical principles.

4 - MAKE PRODUCTIVE USE OF YOUR TIME

Do not love sleep, or you will become poor; open your eyes and you will be satisfied with food. Proverbs 20:13

This Scripture tells us to make productive use of our time, sleeping as we need to, but refusing to "love sleep" to the place where it dominates our lives. If I had to put it into my own words, I'd say, "Don't be too fond of sleep or you will end up in the poorhouse." If you discipline yourself to start each day at a reasonable hour, and diligently work through that day, then there will be food on your table at night, and an inheritance and a legacy for your children's children. I've known many a family where the truth of Proverbs 19:15 came to unfold:

Laziness casts into a deep sleep, and an idle man will suffer hunger.

5 - BECOME SKILLED AT WHAT YOU DO

Do you see a man skilled in his work? He will stand before kings; He will not stand before obscure men. Proverbs 22:29

Observe people who are good at their work — skilled workers are always in demand and admired. Joseph is a great Scriptural example of one who

---

5 - Longman III, Tremper, "Proverbs," 2007, pgs 443; Grand Rapids, MI, Baker Academic.
6 - Bullock, C. Hassell, "An Introduction to the Poetic Books of the Bible", 2007, Moody Publishers

faithfully served his master and eventually blessed the entire land of Egypt with his administrative skills during the seven year famine–and he was only thirty years old when he was appointed!

Now Joseph was thirty years old when he stood before Pharaoh, king of Egypt. And Joseph went out from the presence of Pharaoh and went through all the land of Egypt. Genesis 41:46

Joseph knew that Egypt would have good harvests for seven years so he prudently put portions of those crops away for the coming seven years of famine. Joseph knew the condition of his harvest and put something away for that day.

Know well the condition of your flocks, and pay attention to your herds; for riches are not forever, nor does a crown endure to all generations. When the grass disappears, the new growth is seen, and the herbs of the mountains are gathered in, the lambs will be for your clothing, and the goats will bring the price of a field, and there will be goats' milk enough for your food, for the food of your household, and sustenance for your maidens. Proverbs 27:23-27

Said another way, Joseph had enough sense not to eat all the harvest, and certainly, not to eat the seed corn. Instead, he made sure that plenty of seed was planted to produce more harvests to be stored up for the times of drought.

Proverbs aims to teach the ordinary person how to be wise. This does not mean that all of us will grow to have the spectacular insights of Joseph, but we can all live prudent, upright lives, and we can also become people with active, inquisitive minds. The basis for all wisdom, however, is and always will remain the fear of the Lord.

How many of us fail to practice that biblical principle in our own personal lives, or in our businesses? How many of us spend every penny of our paycheck and have to borrow before the next one arrives? How many businesses spend every dollar that comes in and refuse to plan for a downturn in the economy (yes, downturns are just as predictable as the upturns).

Know the condition of your business. Know the condition of your workplace so that one day you do not go to your desk and suddenly discover...

Behold, it was completely overgrown with thistles; its surface was covered with nettles, and its stone wall was broken down. Proverbs 24:31

Do not let your responsibilities at work become overgrown with weeds and thick with thistles, with all of the fences broken down. As you become careless in your area, you literally create an opportunity for your area of responsibility to fail.

So now let Me tell you what I am going to do to My vineyard: I will remove its hedge and it will be consumed; I will break down its wall and it will become trampled ground. Isaiah 5:5

Riches are not forever. Good times are not forever. Only skilled businessmen, like Joseph, dare to plan for famines and are clever enough to set aside money for the unpredictable future. Because of his planning, Egypt survived to create a legacy as a country. Because of your planning, your family can enjoy a legacy of abundance and prosperity, and you can leave an inheritance to your children's children.

Chapter 3

HOW TO BECOME WISE

What does it mean to possess "biblical wisdom"?

What are you doing to biblically manage your wealth?

When do you possess a healthy "fear of the Lord"?

Why does self-promotion tend towards failure?

How consistent is your effort to seek out the things of God instead of the things of the world?

Why is it important to filter what you say in the workplace? Personal life? Why does the Bible encourage you to respect authority?

In truth, wisdom has little to do with knowing facts.

The proverbs of Solomon, the son of David, king of Israel: To know wisdom and instruction, to discern the sayings of understanding, to receive instruction in wise behavior, righteousness, justice and equity; to give prudence to the naive, to the youth knowledge and discretion, a wise man will hear and increase in learning, and a man of understanding will acquire wise counsel, to understand a proverb and a figure, the words of the wise and their riddles. Proverbs 1:1-6

A man appeared on a national television show not too long ago who was billed as the smartest man in the world. He possessed a photographic memory and had memorized a complete set of encyclopedias. This fellow could dutifully tell you facts about anything: how a hummingbird flies, how an ant digs a tunnel, and how millions of invisible microscopic bugs occupy the beds of every American bedroom—and there was nothing we could do about it!

But let me ask you this: Is that man really smart, or has he simply accumulated more facts than the rest of us in his lifetime thanks to his photographic memory? I believe we often confuse the possession or mastering of facts by a person as intelligence, as wisdom, as the sign of a wise man. If a person reads a book and takes a test on its contents, but fails to answer 30 of 100 questions correctly, we say, "He is barely average." Yet, if that same person re-studies, takes the test again, and only misses 2 questions, we then say, "He is a smart man." But has that person really gained in intelligence or wisdom?

Absolutely not! That person has simply memorized the facts for the test in a more efficient manner the second time around. In truth, wisdom has little to do with knowing facts; the only true way to know what constitutes real wisdom is to consult God's Word.

The two-fold purpose of the book of Proverbs is:

1 Produce the skill of Godly living through wisdom and instruction.
2 Develop discernment and prudence to the "naïve" and ignorant.

The root of "naïve" is a word meaning "an open door," an apt description of the undiscerning who do not know what to keep in or out of their minds. Knowledge and discernment are produced as one ponders the circumstances and avoids sin, thus making a responsible choice.

Not surprisingly, the biblical description of a man who manifests wisdom differs significantly from the world's definition, demanding far more from us as individuals than the accumulation of facts from an encyclopedia to be called smart or wise.

A WISE PERSON LEARNS AND KEEPS ON LEARNING

A wise man will hear and increase in learning and a man of understanding will acquire wise counsel to understand a proverb and a figure, the words of the wise and their riddles. Proverbs 1:5-6

3 - HOW TO BECOME WISE / **49**

One biblical criteria for wisdom is that we "increase in learning" and seek "wise counsel to understand." Even if you are a seasoned journeyman in your profession or an experienced businessman, the quest for true biblical wisdom compels you to constantly seek the counsel and the suggestions of others. I call it seeking fresh wisdom from seasoned men and women who may have developed a different perspective than you have on how to accomplish something.

Proverbs 9:9 puts it this way: *"Give instruction to a wise man and he will be still wiser, teach a righteous man and he will increase his learning."* Do you see the emphasis on constantly growing "wiser" and the need to "increase" the wisdom we currently have? The wise man will receive instruction and be taught from even the least likely person so that he can become ever wiser, adding and evaluating from all sources to broaden his learning.

Friend, do not assume that you know all there is to know in your field, that you have reached the wisdom pinnacle in your trade or profession. You can always learn much more from others! Here is a scriptural, huge caution for all of us:

Do not be wise in your own eyes; fear the LORD and turn away from evil. Proverbs 3:7

Do you see it? The moment you stop learning and start believing that you are too wise to learn from others is when you will start to decline in wisdom. The moment you do not fear evil, but start to figure, "I can handle that temptation," is the moment you will begin to enter into the deceptive, degenerating, captive grips of sin.

The problem with lazy people, and probably the reason they perpetuate their self-destructive behavior, is that they are wise in their own eyes, and as such, unwilling to hear and accept the criticisms or suggestions of others.

As you acquire wisdom, let it ruminate within your mind until you begin to arrive at understanding.

The beginning of wisdom is: acquire wisdom; and with all your acquiring, get understanding. Proverbs 4:7

This is a huge revelation! Acquiring wisdom is the first step, but allowing that wisdom to sink into your spirit and into practice is the only way that it will result in understanding. Meditate upon it; pray about it; ask the Holy Spirit to clarify all the subtle points you are learning. That process will produce seasoned understanding, which becomes the practical, applied wisdom in your life that will benefit you personally, bless your family, and improve your business.

Buy truth, and do not sell it, get wisdom and instruction and understanding. Proverbs 23:23

This verse urges us to "buy truth" at all costs, and then, not to relinquish it at any price!

A WISE PERSON ACCUMULATES WISDOM & MONEY

The crown of the wise is their riches, but the folly of fools is foolishness. Proverbs 14:24

The wise man or woman applies the Scriptural foundations for obtaining wealth, and in the process, accumulates both wealth and the wisdom to take care of it (meaning not spend it all, but wisely put some into investments and savings). On the other hand, fools just get stupider and poorer by the day. As the wise man grows in his riches, he experiences no sorrow with his wealth since he manages his hard-earned money according to God's biblical principles.

It is the blessing of the LORD that makes rich, and He adds no sorrow to it. Proverbs 10:22

The wise man or woman works diligently, and that process generally produces wealth. In the above verse, we see that the blessing of the Lord can bring wealth into our lives. He can bring the wealth through our diligence, or through His blessings, or a combination of both; there is no inconsistency in either process, since He is always the Source, the Provider, the One Who Blesses. Psalm 127:2 emphasizes this same point:

It is vain for you to rise up early, to retire late, to eat the bread of painful labors; for He gives to His beloved even in his sleep.

When God wants to bless you, He will, even when you are sleeping! That does not mean you do not maintain a diligent lifestyle, working hard and in a biblical manner to provide for you and your loved ones. However, when you add to it the supernatural power of God almighty, He can multiply your efforts far beyond what you could ever produce or imagine.

A WISE PERSON FLEES FROM EVIL

Another fundamental principle every wise man and woman must learn and apply in their life is to "fear the LORD and turn away (literally run, as Joseph did from temptation, leaving his coat behind) from evil."

The fear of the LORD is to hate evil; pride and arrogance and the evil way and the perverted mouth, I hate. Proverbs 8:13

How do you develop a healthy fear of the Lord? By reading His Holy Word every day, by learning what brings anger to the Lord, by discerning how He reacts to sin and evil, by understanding how God expects and demands our obedience, and by avoiding the worship of strange idols (modern day idols include, but are not limited to, money, free time, sports, movies, and entertainment). When you read God's Word, any pride and arrogance in your life starts to die, and you begin to replace those faults with godly humility, refusing to be wise in your own estimation (Romans 12:16). Arrogance must be replaced by humility.

Job, considered by most to be one of the wisest men in the Bible, fully grasped this concept when he declared, in the midst of his trials and tribulations, "Behold, the fear of the Lord, that is wisdom; and to depart from evil is understanding." (Job 28:28)

A wise man is cautious and turns away from evil, but a fool is arrogant and careless. The wise watch their steps and avoid evil; fools are headstrong and reckless. Proverbs 22:3 declares:

The prudent sees the evil and hides himself, but the naive go on, and are punished for it.

A WISE PERSON IS HUMBLE

Though He scoffs at the scoffers, yet He gives grace to the afflicted. Proverbs 3:34

God does not approve of those who are scoffers, those who make fun of others. If you are putting down your coworkers, you can expect God to give you a cold shoulder in return. However, if you are down on your luck, just struggling to pay the bills but giving an honest day's labor in your profession, then He will be right by your side waiting to help you because "He gives grace to the afflicted." God is stern to the arrogant, and kind to the humble. The one who chooses his own way arrogantly claims that he knows better than God.

In His Word, God expresses how He expects us to act around others in the workplace: "God is opposed to the proud, but gives grace to the humble" (James 4:6). He virtually repeats that same statement again in 1 Peter 5:5, emphasizing how important this spiritual concept is to Him. Whenever God repeats a biblical principle, it means "Hey there, pay attention to this particular principle – it is absolutely vital to your material and spiritual success."

When others compliment you at work, say "Thank you," and, if the statement properly applies, freely give credit to your coworkers who were involved in the project. Never say, "Well of course it went well, I did it." That display of pride will turn other people in the office off, but far more importantly, you will have God in opposition to your life because "God is opposed to the proud." You probably have noticed that the more wise leaders on a sports team practice this principle after an important win. When interviewed, the winning quarterback will frequently declare, "Our offensive line did an incredible job, and they made my job easy. I had all kinds of time to find my receivers."

A WISE PERSON RECEIVES HONOR – GOD'S WAY

Many businessmen and women strive to receive the respect and honor of their peers in their community. To do this, they plan crazy, attention-getting schemes to win accolades from others. Instead of extravagant displays to attract attention, God offers another path to true honor:

The wise will inherit honor, but fools display dishonor.
Proverbs 3:35

As a man strives to live a wise life (according to biblical standards), then God will reward him with honor, without him having to promote himself one iota! Stupid, contrived schemes of self-promotion and display will only produce futility. Countless public officials have been exposed of attempting to promote themselves through lies and deceit, such as falsifying a graduation certificate to Harvard, or claiming to have been decorated with certain medals from their war service (sometimes they did not even serve!). Such self-promotion ultimately leads to failure. Daniel 12:3 teaches this same principle in a slightly different way, declaring that the wise will ultimately receive glory for what they are—bright lights: *Those who have insight will shine brightly like the brightness of the expanse of heaven...*

A WISE PERSON SEEKS WISDOM, NOT WEALTH!

So many work every day for wealth and financial gain, thinking, very sincerely, that money is the reason they work. We have come to believe, in America, that the paying of the bills and the accumulation of material possessions are the focus of our daily efforts. This belief is the so-called "work ethic" of America, but that belief does not line up very well with Scripture. According to God's Word, the real pursuit that we should be engaging in each day is not to acquire wealth, but to engage in a constant quest to acquire godly wisdom.

For wisdom is better than jewels; and all desirable things cannot compare with her. Proverbs 8:11

As Christian workers and business owners, we need to remember and focus on this Scriptural fact:

wisdom is better than all the trappings wealth can bring – new cars, larger homes, more vacations, etc. In fact, according to Scripture, nothing you could ever wish for can match the rich rewards of wisdom. The most valuable reality a young person could possibly attain is the insight to order his life by the biblical standard of truth.

Pure gold cannot be given in exchange for it, nor can silver be weighed as its price...and the acquisition of wisdom is above that of pearls. Job 28:15, 18b

As a businessman, through the years I have learned that I would be a fool not to seek out and listen to the wisdom of others. The input of others who have been in business longer than I has helped me on numerous occasions to avoid mistakes. When I am faced with what appears to be a business crisis, I diligently seek the advice of others on how best to handle the situation. Through the years, this practice of seeking the counsel of many has been a key factor in blessing my business and our employees.

A WISE PERSON RECEIVES CORRECTION

The wise of heart will receive commands, but a babbling fool will be ruined. Proverbs 10:8

If you want to be successful in business, it is vital that you know how to take orders from others. We have all worked with a person who, when corrected, blows up and makes some crazy, defensive statement such as, "What the heck do you know, anyway? You've made a ton of mistakes yourself, so why do I have to listen to a jerk like you?"

A wise person knows how to take orders; a man who responds to orders as a "babbling fool" will ultimately face ruin (his boss will surely fire him). This same fool hates correction from others, while a wise man appreciates the courage it takes for another person to honestly input into his or her life. The more one embraces folly, the less one can or will receive any critical input, no matter how valuable it might be. However, if a man strives to become wise, he will be open to receive the criticism of others, knowing that it is possible that the input could increase his wisdom.

"Do not reprove a scoffer, or he will hate you, reprove a wise man and he will love you" Proverbs 9:8

Matthew 13:12-16 explains the entire process in a powerful way:

For whoever has, to him more shall be given, and he will have an abundance; but whoever does not have, even what he has shall be taken away from him. Therefore I speak to them in parables; because while seeing they do not see, and while hearing they do not hear, nor do they understand. In their case the prophecy of Isaiah is being fulfilled, which says, "You will keep on hearing, but will not understand; You will keep on seeing, but will not perceive; For the heart of this people has become dull, With their ears they scarcely hear, and they have closed their eyes, otherwise they would see with their eyes, hear with their ears, and understand with their heart and return, and I would heal them." But blessed are your eyes, because they see; and your ears, because they hear.

Jesus considered it important for us to hear His words, to receive His corrections, and to act on His instructions.

Therefore everyone who hears these words of Mine and acts on them, may be compared to a wise man who built his house on the rock. Matthew 7:24

A WISE PERSON CONTROLS HIS TONGUE

Imagine the same babbling fool we just met has been given an assignment he does not want to do. He may respond something like this: "Why do I always have to clean up after the carpenters? They leave such a mess. Why not have Dave do it? He gets all the good jobs. I'm sick of being the clean-up guy."

By failing to control his mouth, the babbling fool releases the seeds of his own destruction, and ultimately, of his likely firing, or the failure of his business. Longman states, "Talking too much leads to all kinds of problems. It is not that wise people never speak, it is that they choose their words very carefully."[7] The fool self-destructs. The hearer judges from what is said whether the person speaking is wise or a fool. The words flowing from our mouths usually inform the hearer of what is going on inside of us.

Wise men store up knowledge, but with the mouth of the foolish, ruin is at hand. Proverbs 10:14

The wise learn how to accumulate knowledge — the real treasure in life. They do not learn for just the moment, but in preparation for the future. It is wise and prudent to control and filter the knowledge that you do have until a time that is appropriate to act. In doing so, you demonstrate that you are knowledgeable in a given area. If you do not see yourself growing in wisdom, it is likely you have not made it a priority, seeking it with diligence. The wise person is a model of restraint and humility, speaking what he knows at the right time.

Examine yourself and see if you are not placing too much importance upon distractions that are like fool's gold. Determine to focus your mind and heart on seeking the lasting treasures of God, which will lead to joy and a successful future.

---

7 - Longman III, Tremper, "Proverbs," 2007, pg 284; Grand Rapids, MI, Baker Academic.

The wise learn how to control their tongues, and not act like a know-it-all when they are given correction. The fool continues to prove his foolishness by babbling when given orders and by complaining when given assignments.

This area is so important and fundamental that I have included here several other Scriptures for you to study. I hope that as you do, if you have a problem with your tongue, these Scriptures will convict you of the necessity to bring your words under control!

The one who guards his mouth preserves his life [business or job]; *the one who opens wide his lips comes to ruin.* Proverbs 13:3

A fool's mouth is his ruin, and his lips are the snare of his soul. Proverbs 18:7

Fools carelessly provide the ammunition for their own destruction and ruin. This prophecy could demonstrate itself in many ways, including false promises or assertions, discourse, lies, and many other verbal traps. The eventual ruin of a fool could come financially, socially, physically, spiritually, or a combination of all four areas.

The tongue of the wise makes knowledge acceptable, but the mouth of fools spouts folly. Proverbs 15:2

Knowledge flows like spring water from the wise, but fools are leaky faucets, dripping nonsense. Bridges says, "Wisdom is shown not by the quantity of knowledge, but by applying it in the right way."[8]

The lips of the wise spread knowledge, but the hearts of fools are not so. Proverbs 15:7

---

8 - Bridges, Charles, "An Exposition On the Book of Proverbs," 1847, page 174; Carlisle, PA, 17013, Banner of Truth Publications.

If you take care of your outlook and attitude towards life, your influence will take care of itself.

A prudent man conceals knowledge, but the heart of fools proclaims folly. Proverbs 12:23

A fool always gives himself away, as well as any secret ever entrusted to him. Every prudent man acts with knowledge, but a fool displays folly. Proverbs 13:16

A wise person tends to be reflective and to think before he or she answers; fools tend to be impulsive and speak without thinking or filtering their thoughts. Charles Bridges puts it this way: "We must think twice before we speak once."[9]

The heart of the righteous ponders how to answer, but the mouth of the wicked pours out evil things. Proverbs 15:28

In a study of Scripture, when a topic is constantly repeated, that is a good indication of its importance. The Scriptures above are just some of the ones in Proverbs that speak about controlling the tongue. If I were to also include Scriptures from others parts of the Bible that urge control of the tongue, it would take another book. This key spiritual principle is vital for the proper balance in our personal lives, in our marriages, in our work environments, and in running our businesses.

A WISE MAN'S WEALTH PROVIDES PROTECTION

The rich man's wealth is his fortress, the ruin of the poor is their poverty. Proverbs 10:15

Wealth is not just for the accumulation of material things and new toys. Wealth can provide a covering, an insulation for the ups and downs of

---

9 - Bridges, Charles, "An Exposition On the Book of Proverbs," 1847, Page 104; Carlisle, PA, 17013, Banner of Truth Publications.

life. Wealth can serve as a fortress, a bastion from a fluctuating and unstable economy, providing a level of security for the wealthy man's family.

Poverty, on the other hand, does not offer much in the way of positive protective elements! The indigent struggle daily for food and shelter, and they do not have the ability to provide for their families, or for their health. Poverty ultimately can lead to ruin. That is why Proverbs 18:11 declares:

A rich man's wealth is his strong city, and like a high wall in his own imagination.

Along with the qualities of obtaining wealth, God's Word also offers an important caution: do not trust in our wealth as our refuge, but recognize God as the source of all the wealth in our lives. God gives wealth, and He can take it away, so the only true trust we can have is in Him!

Behold, the man who would not make God his refuge, but trusted in the abundance of his riches and was strong in his evil desire. Psalm 52:7

A WISE PERSON PLEASES HIS PARENTS (BOSS OR AUTHORITY)

A wise son makes a father glad, but a foolish man despises his mother. Proverbs 15:20

Wise children make their parents very proud; conversely, lazy students or disrespectful children embarrass their parents. As mothers and fathers, it is important to recognize our children when they are doing well with praise and compliments. However, it is also important that when they have displays of foolishness that we lovingly correct them and still let them feel our love rather than rejection. A foolish child can cause grief, but when he is in the process of developing, it is important that we temper the grief with loving correction. Solomon wrote, *A wise son makes a father glad, but a foolish son is a grief to his mother.* Proverbs 10:1

God, in His Word, has always placed a very high premium on how a wise child can bring honor to his parents.

A man who loves wisdom makes his father glad, but he who keeps company with harlots wastes his wealth. Proverbs 29:3

If you are an employee, here is an interesting exercise: substitute the word "boss" or "authority" for "father" or "mother" in the above Scriptures. You will find that as you respect authority, the same blessings will come upon you, and you will bless your boss. Conversely, if you are constantly the one in the workplace who is attacking management, you may consider this Scripture:

The eye that mocks a father and scorns a mother, the ravens of the valley will pick it out, and the young eagles will eat it. Proverbs 30:17

It is important to remember that God has a specific perspective on authority, and He calls on us to embrace that same perspective. To help mold that perspective into God's spiritual perspective, here are a few other Scriptures about sons where you can substitute "son" or "child" with "employee" and substitute "father" with "boss" or "authority" to begin to receive a new perspective about your role in the workplace.

My son, if your heart is wise, my own heart also will be glad. Proverbs 23:15

The biblical motivation given to the son to grow in wisdom comes back as a blessing to the parents as they see their children grow into godly people.

Be wise, my son, and make my heart glad, that I may reply to him who reproaches me. Proverbs 27:11

Listen, my son, and be wise, and direct your heart in the way. Proverbs 23:19

A WISE PERSON SPEAKS SOFTLY

So often in the business world a person who speaks softly is considered an easy mark for the more aggressive and vocal competitors. But Scripture does not agree with that worldly assessment. Proverbs 16:21 teaches us:

The wise in heart will be called understanding, and sweetness of speech increases persuasiveness.

Contrary to worldly beliefs and teachings, "sweetness of speech" is a vital key to friendly persuasion; yelling, screaming and acting generally like a maniac causes people to block you out or discount your message. A wise person becomes known for his insight, and his gracious words add to his reputation.

The heart of the wise instructs his mouth and adds persuasiveness to his lips. Proverbs 16:23

Wise men are persuasive whenever they speak, and as they speak, their reputation increases, But the mouth of the wicked pours out evil things. Proverbs 15:28

The mouth of the righteous utters wisdom, and his tongue speaks justice. Proverbs 37:30

The righteous, wise person generally speaks

when necessary, and can be both constructive and lovingly critical when appropriate, is helpful to others, and has the ability to clean up the messes in the office caused by fools. The fool, on the other hand, generally does not listen well or respond favorably to constructive criticism, talks too much, causes trouble, lacks emotional maturity, and for some reason, seems to enjoy stirring up trouble.

Another way to spot the difference between a fool and a wise man is in how much they divulge of what they know. A fool has a tendency to tell you everything he knows; be it office gossip, problems with another worker, etc. A wise man uses a verbal filter, and will seriously consider what he says, being careful not to release information that could cause harm or create conflict with the office atmosphere.

When a wise man encounters a controversy or conflict with a foolish man, the foolish man either rages or laughs, and there is no rest in the business office. When a wise man tries to work things out with a fool, he receives only scorn and sarcasm for his trouble. In the midst of these situations, it is up to the wise man to set the standard for behavior in the work atmosphere.

A fool always loses his temper, but a wise man holds it back. Proverbs 29:11

What is anger? I believe it could be described as temporary madness. Take time to weigh the offense so as not to rise to quick anger; try not to think of the offense in the worse possible light at the moment, but take the time to calm down inside before reacting.

A fool lets his emotions vomit all over those around him; a wise sage quietly mulls over the problem without displaying rage or anger that causes discord. By controlling his emotions, the wise man can generally help prevent potential explosive situations from escalating. So many men are spending their lifetimes in prison because they were quick to anger instead of taking the time to calm down before reacting to a perceived offense.

A man's discretion makes him slow to anger, and it is his glory to overlook a transgression. Proverbs 19:11

A WISE PERSON FINDS WISDOM

Wisdom is too exalted for a fool, he does not open his mouth in the gate. Proverbs 24:7

Wisdom is out of the reach of a fool; in a serious discussion, the fool is lost because he has not been able to obtain wisdom. Proverbs 14:6 shares, *A scoffer seeks wisdom and finds none, but knowledge is easy to one who has understanding.* Who has understanding? A person who obtains wisdom, and then meditates upon that wisdom until it evolves into practical understanding. A fool is totally incapable of such maturity in his actions.

Wisdom is in the presence of the one who has understanding, but the eyes of a fool are on the ends of the earth. Proverbs 17:24

The perceptive (the wise) can find wisdom in their own front yards; fools look for it everywhere but right where it is – in front of their noses!

The wise man's eyes are in his head, but the fool walks in darkness and yet I know that one fate befalls them both. Ecclesiastes 2:14

There is so much in Scripture about the poor fools and their lives. Proverbs 21:20 says that even when a fool has wisdom in his house, he "swallows it up." You see, spiritual valuables are safe in the possession of a wise man; a fool fails to recognize the valuable treasures in his own home and puts them out to spiritual yard sales.

The failure of a fool lies at their own door. Charles Bridges observes the truth of that statement in describing the process one follows to become a fool:

"He seeks but without seriousness, without honesty, without delight, and solely for his own interest. Therefore, he finds matters enough for his humor, but not for his instruction."[10]

A WISE PERSON IS STRONGER

A wise man is strong, and a man of knowledge increases power. Proverbs 24:5

I love that scripture! If you are ever asked, "Is it better to be wise or strong?" always answer, "It is better to be wise." Intelligence outranks muscle any day!

A wise man scales the city of the mighty and brings down the stronghold in which they trust. Proverbs 21:22

A WISE PERSON STRIVES TO WIN SOULS

The fruit of the righteous is a tree of life, and he who is wise wins souls. Proverbs 11:30

A good life is a spiritual life; we are all called to be fruit-bearing spiritual trees, and the spiritual fruit we are all called to produce is souls!

Those who have insight will shine brightly like the brightness of the expanse of heaven, and those who lead the many to righteousness, like the stars forever and ever. Daniel 12:3

---

10 - Bridges, Charles, "An Exposition On the Book of Proverbs," 1847, Page 104; Carlisle, PA, 17013, Banner of Truth Publications.

Paul wrote a potent, powerful passage that perfectly describes what we are all called to be in the workplace and in our personal lives – soul winners!

For though I am free from all men, I have made myself a slave to all, so that I may win more. To the Jews I became as a Jew, so that I might win Jews; to those who are under the Law, as under the Law though not being myself under the Law, so that I might win those who are under the Law; to those who are without law, as without law, though not being without the law of God but under the law of Christ, so that I might win those who are without law. To the weak I became weak, that I might win the weak; I have become all things to all men, so that I may by all means save some. 1 Corinthians 9:19-22

Paul became all things to all men so that he might by "all means save some." If we are to be wise men and women, according to God's Word, then we are called to do whatever it takes to win souls, even if it means becoming "weak" to win the weak. In your work environment, that may mean humbling yourself in a situation so another person can grow to trust you. There are a multitude of scenarios of how the Holy Spirit will direct you in the workplace, but the bottom line is this: a wise man becomes a witness in order to win souls, through God's grace, for His Kingdom!

Let him know that he who turns a sinner from the error of his way will save his soul from death and will cover a multitude of sins. James 5:20

Chapter 4

MORE THAN MONEY
TO TRULY BE RICH

Describe the difference between being wealthy and being rich, according to the guidelines in Proverbs.

What does it mean to say that "money is but a small ingredient" of true wealth or poverty?

Do you, or someone you know, flaunt your wealth? How do others react to these displays?

According to biblical principles, how can one scatter wealth, yet increase it?

What does contentment mean to you?
How much time do you spend seeking thrills and how much time seeking God?

Which is better, a good reputation or wealth? Explain your answer.

...money is but a small ingredient of wealth or poverty.

Probably no word is more misunderstood in today's society than "riches." To many, maybe even most, it simply means having more money than you will ever need. However, according to Proverbs, it takes much more than mere wealth to become truly rich. Proverbs shares how certain godly behaviors are necessary, along with the wealth, to produce a quality of life that manifests true riches and values. The life and death of one prominent billionaire demonstrates the reality of that biblical assessment for true riches.

WEALTHY BUT NOT RICH

Leona Helmsley and her third husband, Harry, ran a $5 billion hotel empire that also included managing the Empire State Building. She circled the globe in a 100-seat private jet with a bedroom suite; her numerous residences included a nine-room penthouse with a swimming pool overlooking Central Park and an $8 million estate in Connecticut.

Yet, she was known to nickel-and-dime merchants on her personal purchases, often arguing over amounts as small as $4.00; she also had a reputation for refusing to pay contractors who worked on her commercial and personal projects the previously agreed amounts. Her hired help and hotel executives constantly quit her employment due to her apparently well-earned reputation as the queen of mean and to her demeaning nature.

In 1989 she was tried for tax evasion; ex-employees gleefully testified against her, describing how she terrorized both the menial and executive help at her homes and hotels. One quoted her as saying, "We don't pay taxes. Only the little people pay taxes." After an eight-week trial, Mrs. Helmsley was convicted of evading $1.2 million in federal taxes and sentenced to four years in the federal prison.

Leona Helmsley's $2.5 billion fortune certainly made her wealthy, but she was not rich according to the principles in Proverbs. Upon her death, she was described by the media as a "cutthroat hotel magnate" and the "queen of mean". She died alienated from her dead son's wife (she actually sued his estate!); she cut two of her four grandchildren out of her will, yet left $12 million to her dog! Her time in prison, her family divisions and her legal problems amply demonstrated the truth of Proverbs 11:4: *Riches do not profit in the day of wrath, but righteousness delivers from death.*

Mrs. Helmsley's thick bankroll was of no help to her at all when her family and her two previous marriages started to fall apart. Because she did not live a principled, righteous life – obeying the laws of both God and man - she endured public humiliation, personal embarrassment, and ultimately, prison for her crimes. Had Mrs. Helmsley read and practiced Proverbs 10:2, she would have avoided the tax manipulations that landed her in jail:

Ill-gotten gains do not profit, but righteousness delivers from death.

Clearly, there is a difference between wealth and riches. Wealth is simply the accumulation of money;

riches involves a quality of life that comes from living a godly life, manifesting biblical values. Let me illustrate the difference with two simple questions.

If I asked you, "Do you want to be wealthy?" you'd probably say, "Heck, yeah, who doesn't?" But if I asked you, "Do you want to live the life of Leona Helmsley?" you'd probably answer, "Absolutely not."

Great wealth is in the house of the righteous, but trouble is in the income of the wicked. Proverbs 15:6

Are you beginning to see the difference between wealth and riches? Mrs. Helmsley was indeed wealthy beyond measure, but it takes more than money to be rich in God's plan. When they placed Mrs. Helmsley to rest, her survivors should have placed this Scripture on her urn or tombstone:

Better is a little with righteousness than great income with injustice. Proverbs 16:8

In this chapter I want to share some of the biblical truths you need to know, possess and practice to not just be wealthy, but to be truly rich in God's Kingdom.

1 - DON'T BE A SHOW OFF

If you are currently in the process of building wealth, God's Word cautions that you need to be careful how you display that wealth to others.

There is one who pretends to be rich, but has nothing; another pretends to be poor, but has great wealth. Proverbs 13:7

A pretentious, showy lifestyle produces nothing but an empty life. The manifestation of a plain, simple life best allows the money you have to help you become truly rich. When a person begins to believe that the latest new Cadillac and the big $5 million mansion are the necessary material things that define him, his life starts to become shallow and empty – wrapped up in meaningless things rather than matters of spiritual substance. This verse is a reminder that both subjectively and objectively money is but a small ingredient of wealth or poverty.

If you are wealthy now, know that it is far better to enjoy your wealth without flaunting it. You do not need to drive a brand new Bentley Azure automobile to prove you are rich; there are many other nicely equipped cars that will provide you with a wonderful ride, a great sound system, and do not cost $324,000 to purchase.

When you start to fall into that trap of needing to flagrantly demonstrate your wealth to others, your life is destined to become empty. There will always be someone else with a more expensive car or home (yes, there are more expensive cars than the Azure), and someone will always wear a bigger diamond ring than the one you put on your wife's finger to showcase your wealth.

One recent example of how flaunting wealth or pretending to be wealthier than you are can lead to ruin was the fate of Brazilian billionaire Eike Batista. In 2012, he was reputed to be the seventh-richest man in the world. In October of 2013, his flagship oil company, OGX, filed for bankruptcy with a debt estimated at more than $800 million. Many Brazilians, long since soured on his cocky persona, expensive mansions, his fleet of airplanes and yachts, responded with glee on social networks to the news that Batista's yacht, the Pink Fleet, would soon be sold for scrap because no one wanted, or could afford, the $19-million boat intact (it originally cost $35 million to build).

Batista's much-hyped empire was built mainly

on vastly overconfident assumptions—in particular, the worth of oil deposit estimates that bore no relationship to reality. "He ended up swallowed by his own myth," one Brazilian columnist wrote. Much of his fabulous wealth was based upon little more than promises and false assumptions.

One close associate declared that Batista's "vanity prevailed over common sense." Amid Batista's opulent lifestyle and assurances of big gains, each of Batista's companies had the letter X in its title, signifying multiple returns. His personal fortune soared, even as the companies brought in little revenue.

Batista, a one-time powerboat racer, favored fast cars and large yachts. For years, he kept a Lamborghini and a silver Mercedes-Benz SLR McLaren in his living room. Those showy riches are now a small comfort to the man who made and lost $28 billion in a heartbeat. Clearly, Batista pretended to be wealthier than he was, using shell money based upon promises, to create an appearance of success to lure investors, and to finance his vain, extravagant lifestyle.

2 - GIVING AWAY MONEY INCREASES RICHES

This truth is diametrically opposed to what seems logical from the world's eyes. The world essentially teaches, "Get all you can, can all you get, then sit on the can." That seemed to be the motto Leona Helmsley, "the Queen of Mean," followed on her way to accumulating worldly wealth. But God's Word has a different approach, one that essentially declares, "The more money you give away to bless others, the more God will flow His abundance back into your life." Proverbs 11:24-26 says it this way:
There is one who scatters, and yet increases all the more, and there is one who withholds what is justly

due, and yet it results only in want. The generous man will be prosperous, and he who waters will himself be watered. He who withholds grain, the people will curse him, but blessing will be on the head of him who sells it.

How can you scatter, yet increase? Only through the grace of God and by following His wisdom and counsel to freely plant sacred seeds into the Gospel through your tithes and offerings. How can you withhold and still be in want? The direct result of hoarding can be a loss of the wealth being tucked away. Dr. H.A. Ironside quotes a quaint rhyme by John Bunyan to emphasize this principle that goes like this:

"A man there was, though some thought mad, the more he gave away, the more he had. He that bestows his goods upon the poor, Still has as much again, and ten times more."[11]

Proverbs teaches that generosity is a quality trait of the wise. This teaching, however, does not mean Proverbs is advocating that a businessman or woman carelessly invest in business ventures to the exclusion of the prudent principle of building up a reserve account for emergencies.

God has given us extra money to bless others. God has designed us to be other-centered, and when we structure our financial lives focused solely on our own needs, that life becomes one destined to suffer poverty in the things of God.

But God said to him, "You fool! This very night your soul is required of you; and now who will own what you have prepared?" So is the man who stores up treasure for himself, and is not rich toward God. Luke 12:20-21

The selfish, wealthy person "is not rich toward God," and being "rich toward God" is the only type of

---

11 - Bunyan, John, "The Pilgrim's Progress" 1678, social-texts.com Part Two : Section VII http://www.sacred-texts.com/chr/bunyan/pp18.htm

riches that really means anything. That is why Jesus declared in Luke 12:33,

"Sell your possessions and give to charity; make yourselves money belts which do not wear out, an unfailing treasure in heaven, where no thief comes near nor moth destroys."

The only treasure that cannot fail is the one built up in the heavenly places.

3 - PEOPLE FLOCK TO SUCCESSFUL PEOPLE

It is God's desire that you have an impact on those in your circle of influence for His glory. To best do this, it is helpful to recognize that people gravitate toward successful people. God wants to use your wealth and status to attract others so you can hopefully impact their lives for the Gospel.

The poor is hated even by his neighbor, but those who love the rich are many. Proverbs 14:20

This Scripture simply acknowledges a basic human characteristic: we tend to shun those perceived as losers and we tend to gravitate toward those who manifest success and influence upon others. People faithful to God frequently flourish because God knows they will use their power and influence for His Kingdom. Proverbs 19:4 shares this truth as well: *Wealth adds many friends, but a poor man is separated from his friend.*

Wealthy people attract friends as honey draws flies, but poor people are frequently avoided because they are shallowly perceived as people who cannot offer value to the lives of others. The previous Scripture was not written to justify our worldly behavior, but to explain the cold reality that rests in the unredeemed human nature of all men.

Since it is man's basest nature to seek out and love the rich and successful, as you become rich and flow in the righteousness of God, you can use that basic fact to witness to and bless those who diligently seek you out.

There is an important caution here: never think God's Word values a wealthy man more than a poor one!

The rich and the poor have a common bond, The LORD is the maker of them all. Proverbs 22:2

The rich and the poor shake hands as equals — God made them both. God even declares that when we bless the poor, we bless Him. *He who oppresses the poor taunts his Maker, but he who is gracious to the needy honors Him* Proverbs 14:31. In fact, Scripture declares it is better to be poor and honest than rich and dishonest.

Better is the poor who walks in his integrity than he who is crooked though he be rich. Proverbs 28:6

4 - LESS MONEY AND MORE OF GOD IS BETTER

The real riches are the things of God, so seek Him first. Having a great deal of wealth but no fear of the Lord is futile and fruitless. On the surface, those who are rich and those who are poor have plenty of differences in their lives and normally keep a clear separation in society. However, Proverbs reminds us that the rich and the poor are all human beings, and they are viewed the same by our Creator. A man may walk in a godly way yet be poor, while another man might walk in an ungodly way and be rich. The poor man with all of his material disadvantage can be more honorable and useful than the rich man with all of his earthly possessions.

Better is a little with the fear of the LORD than great treasure and turmoil with it. Proverbs 15:16

I believe the Amplified Bible provides a more detailed translation of this Scripture, since many misunderstand the biblical definition of "fear of the Lord."

Better is little with the reverent, worshipful fear of the Lord than great and rich treasure and trouble with it.

Living a simple life in the "reverent, worshipful fear of the Lord" is far better than rich treasure that is accompanied by constant turmoil and problems. Again, I reference the life of Leona Helmsley and countless others who have made money their major focus, to the exclusion of blessing those around them.

Living a life where you reverence God and worship Him is far better than a life of wealth that is soiled by ungodly actions and principles that produce a ton of headaches. Proverbs 16:8 says the same thing in a slightly different way:

Better is a little with righteousness than great income with injustice.

Of course, Ecclesiastes 4:6 phrases this principle in a way that only Ecclesiastes can: *One hand full of rest is better than two fists full of labor and striving after wind.*

Have you ever met that person who is never satisfied with the amount of money he or she has? In truth, you may be that person. If you are, the amount you have is almost irrelevant. If you have one million, it will now take two million to really make you happy. If you get to two million, you will soon come to realize that it is actually five million that will do the trick. If you are that person, you have wealth but not riches, because 1 Timothy 6:6 tells us, *But godliness actually is a means of great gain when accompanied by contentment.*

When was the last time you actually thought about contentment as a means to great gain and peace? Charles Bridges, in his famous work, *A Commentary on Proverbs*, suggests the following mental filter as a step towards contentment:

"Ponder every thought that may disturb contentment. If you have fewer comforts than you used to have, or fewer comforts than other people have, or fewer comforts than you desire, do you not still have more than you deserve? If you had more (comforts), would you not be tempted to forget God and live in a worldly way?"[12]

5 - WEALTH WITHOUT PEACE IS NOT RICHES

Better is a dry morsel and quietness with it than a house full of feasting with strife. Proverbs 17:1

Friend, a meal of bread and water in contentment and peace is far better than a banquet spiced with quarrels. How many times have you read in the newspaper or heard on the news media the tragic stories of wealthy families locked in bitter, lifetime battles over fortunes and family misunderstandings? Now please do not get me wrong here: poor people can have quarrels and family fractures as well. This Scripture just determines and sets a value priority: seek peace before profit; seek quiet before contention; value family unity with little wealth over family division accompanied by great wealth.

Better is a dish of vegetables where love is than a fattened ox served with hatred. Proverbs 15:17

---

12 - Bridges, Charles, "The Crossway Classic Commentaries, Bridges" 2001, page 139; Wheaton, IL 60187, Good News Publishers.

The fool destroys himself by his idleness, while a person who is too ambitious destroys himself by striving after too much. Moderation is viewed in Scripture as a healthy goal, and adds to the dignity of the person. Moderation is useful for every beneficial activity. If the goal of achieving wealth is overwhelming, and the amount of money is "never enough," dominating a person's life, then the endeavor is truly futile. A little with peace is far better than much in turmoil. Charles Bridges wrote it this way:

"Riches and poverty are more issues of the heart than in the hand. He is wealthy who is contented; he is poor who wants more."[13]

6 - WEALTH IS NOT YOUR PROTECTION – GOD IS

A rich man's wealth is his strong city, and like a high wall in his own imagination. Proverbs 18:11

Many wealthy men and women mistakenly believe that their wealth protects and insulates them from society and the law. They imagine that they are safe behind their huge bank accounts. While it is true that wealth and money can help us navigate some issues and problems in life, it will let us down in the most important, eternal issues. So many wealthy people have demonstrated how false their "protection system" belief is: Leona Helmsley and Martha Stewart are just two of the wealthy people who have gone to prison because their abundant bank accounts could not protect them from their illegal actions.

The rich man's wealth is his fortress, the ruin of the poor is their poverty. Proverbs 10:15

Wealth is fleeting and uncertain. The only real protection we have in this life is through our personal relationship with our Heavenly Father.

---

13 - Bridges, Charles, "The Crossway Classic Commentaries, Bridges" 2001, pages 121, 139; Wheaton, IL 60187, Good News Publishers.

Instruct those who are rich in this present world not to be conceited or to fix their hope on the uncertainty of riches, but on God, who richly supplies us with all things to enjoy. 1 Timothy 6:17

Rather than wearing one's self out pursuing wealth, pursue the wisdom of God and what glorifies Him, and He will bless you with prosperity as He chooses. The person who has dedicated his every waking hour to amassing a fortune is often instantly deprived of all of his wealth in an instant (remember the Brazilian Batista?).

A financial empire can collapse and crash as the result of disease, misjudgment, embezzlement, extravagance, family in-fighting, fraud or theft.

You have probably noticed that the United States dollar bill has an eagle on it. History has proven in countless companies that the eagle can fly away if you are not careful with it. Of course, there is nothing wrong with being rich. However, **do not make wealth a goal in your life because wealth is not a permanent thing you can trust.** A wealthy man once said, "I do not make money for the sake of money, but I make money for what it can do. At first I made money for me, but now I make money for what it can do for God."

7 - WEALTH WITHOUT RELATIONSHIPS IS EMPTY

Leona Helmsley married three times, yet never seemed to enjoy godly family relationships. Scripture maintains that strong relationships with wives, children and others are godly parts of real riches.
House and wealth are an inheritance from fathers, but a prudent wife is from the LORD. Proverbs 19:14

Houses and land can be inherited, handed down

from parents from one generation to another – that is wealth. But a congenial spouse is not an inheritance, and she comes straight from God – that is riches!

A key benefit from solid relationships is that honest people will help you keep a godly perspective, since wealthy men tend to think too highly of themselves.

The rich man is wise in his own eyes, but the poor who has understanding sees through him. Proverbs 28:11

A rich man may be wise in his own eyes, but to a poor man who has discernment, he sees right through the rich man's facade. Being truly wise, and being wise in our own eyes are often confused, though they are essentially opposite traits.

Unfortunately, wealthy people begin to think they know it all, but the poor can see right through their pretense. That is why it is especially important for a wealthy person to stay humble. No one knows it all, and no one appreciates or wants to be around or work for a person who thinks he does.

Do not be wise in your own eyes; fear the LORD and turn away from evil. Proverbs 3:7

The person who is wise in his own eyes (riches can produce pride and conceit) is the person who leans on his own understanding. That kind of wisdom is foolishness and self-delusion. Even a non-Christian could remark, "I suppose that many might have attained to wisdom had they not thought they had already attained it," (Seneca).[14]

In Proverbs, wealth is generally better than poverty, but as people use wealth to self-delude and to delude others, then wealth can be worse than poverty. The expression *in their own eyes* is used in a number of

---

14 - Spurgeon, Charles, "The Saint And His Saviour", 1867, pg 120
(Not original source)

places in Proverbs to emphasize this point.

8 - THE PURSUIT OF PLEASURE WILL NEVER SATISFY

Wealth brings with it the possibility of many amazing things: pricey cars, private jets and yachts, multiple homes, expensive wardrobes and show-off jewelry. Wealth also offers the lure of endless parties and alcohol, an endless supply of drugs for sexual stimulation, drugs for depression, drugs to slow down aging, plastic surgery, and stem-cell therapy. Wealth can buy love in all the wrong places, and can guarantee that virtually any pleasure known to man can be obtained for a price, but that sort of pleasure-seeking wealth ultimately leads to an empty life, a life impoverished of godly values.

He who loves pleasure will become a poor man; he who loves wine and oil will not become rich. Proverbs 21:17

If you are addicted to thrills and pleasures, you are destined to live an empty life! The pursuit of pleasure is never satiated or satisfied; in fact, it constantly demands more and more. This scriptural truth is overwhelmingly documented almost every day in the media as pop stars and divas, actors and actresses continue to check themselves into drug or alcohol rehabilitation clinics, or attempt suicides due to their wealthy but empty, meaningless lifestyles. A restless desire to be rich subjects a person to tremendous spiritual peril.

For the heavy drinker and the glutton will come to poverty and drowsiness will clothe one with rags. Proverbs 23:21

The Apostle Paul warns of the same problem of pursing empty thrills and temporary pleasures from a slightly different angle:

But those who want to get rich fall into temptation and a snare and many foolish and harmful desires which plunge men into ruin and destruction. 1 Timothy 6:9

Clearly, with the accumulation of wealth comes the responsibility to use it wisely, not on "foolish and harmful desires" that will ultimately lead to "ruin and destruction."

9 - HONEST PEOPLE TAKE SURE STEPS

Have you ever been in one of those "trust circles" where a person stands in the middle and falls backwards, forced to trust those behind him that he cannot see to catch him? Well, in the circle of life, there needs to be honest people in our "trust circle" who practice the biblical steps on the road to accumulating wealth and experiencing riches, people we can count on for wisdom, and people we can count on to be there should we fall as we walk through this life.

A wicked man displays a bold face, but as for the upright, he makes his way sure. Proverbs 21:29

Honesty is part of having riches instead of just wealth, and provides a sure way, a sure path. A dishonest person fakes their way through life, and that person is constantly caught in bold-faced lies or inappropriate actions. They are described as "insincere" and "not trustworthy." Most people would never knowingly trust this type of person in a financial transaction (unless they gave that person permission to tell lies on their behalf). On the other hand, honest people are sure of their steps, and they can be described as "reliable" or "trustworthy."

The righteousness of the blameless will smooth his way, but the wicked will fall by his own wickedness. Proverbs 11:5

Too often wicked people will use the good will of a Christian to constantly ask for forgiveness for their offenses, knowing that Christians are commanded to forgive. However, the ancients have the wisdom to declare, "To be repeatedly requesting forgiveness for offenses repeatedly committed is not repentance, but only acceptance." In other words, we are not commanded to forgive a person who proves, by their actions, that they are not repentant.

10 - A GOOD REPUTATION IS BETTER THAN WEALTH

There would be no victims of Mrs. Helmsley's meanness and cutthroat negotiations if she had only read and practiced the truth described in Proverbs 22:1:

A good name is to be more desired than great wealth, favor is better than silver and gold.

According to God's Word, a sterling reputation is far better than striking it rich; a gracious spirit is far better than copious amounts of money in the bank; a person of integrity is worth more and far better to know than a person of wealth.

The memory of the righteous is blessed, but the name of the wicked will rot. Proverbs 10:7

Our Lord carries this teaching a step further in Luke 10:20 to demonstrate that there is still a higher level, nour proper joy is not in wielding power but in the love we are given.

Nevertheless do not rejoice in this, that the spirits are

*"Self discipline weighs ounces;
regret weighs tons."*

Jim Rohn

When you first start reading the Book of Proverbs you will note a very important fact–the words in Proverbs 1:3 speak of the importance of self-control and discipline:

Receive instruction in wise dealing and the discipline of wise thoughtfulness, righteousness, justice, and integrity. (AMP)

Discipline, and its close synonym of "correction" (Proverbs 3:11), both refer to the ability to control oneself and focus on the important tasks at hand, even if other behaviors would be more pleasing and demand less effort.

The reverent and worshipful fear of the Lord is the beginning and the principal and choice part of knowledge [its starting point and its essence]; but fools despise skillful and godly wisdom, instruction, and discipline. Proverbs 1:7 (AMP)

Many biblical scholars believe that when it comes to the challenge of living, Proverbs reveals perhaps the most indispensable tool available to all of us, no matter what our other talents or abilities might be: discipline. Without this simple trait, it is almost impossible to live a productive, satisfying and purposeful life. Proverbs 13:18 declares: *He who ignores discipline comes to poverty and shame.* Those two destinations – poverty and shame – are not places that any sane person would desire to visit!

Yet, for most of us the idea of discipline conjures up stern negative images of a child being spanked, a student being yelled at, a soldier being court-martialed for disobedience, or a thief being sentenced to prison. Or, we think of discipline as an unavoidable evil or a repressive sentence imposed upon our fun lifestyle to restrict our overeating or to slow down our frivolous spending.

In essence, most of us normally think of discipline as a form of deprivation that is destined to make our lives unpleasant, miserable and distasteful! But, there is another way to think about discipline.

For the commandment is a lamp and the teaching is light; and reproofs for discipline are the way of life.
Proverbs 6:23

Scripture declares that discipline can bring "light" into our lives and can improve our "way of life." In his book, *Character Traits of an Athlete*, Bruce Brown writes, "Discipline should not have a negative connotation to the athlete. Discipline is simply focused attention and effort. When it is balanced and done through love, discipline is involved in all athletic successes."[15]

As we study Proverbs on the subject of discipline, we will see that it is God's heart that His discipline, done through love, manifests and produces an empowering discipline into our lives that helps us achieve success in both the spiritual realm and in the natural realm.

---

15 - Brown, Bruce, "Teaching Character Through Sport : Developing A Positive Coaching Legacy" 2003

Apply your heart to discipline and your ears to words of knowledge. Proverbs 23:12

As your heart is open to godly, empowering discipline, your life can dramatically change, and your knowledge will increase. Dr. Morris Cerullo, a Christian teacher and evangelist, frequently declares in his books that "All truths are parallel."[16] In that declaration, he is teaching that there are strong parallels between the natural world and the spiritual realm. That is plainly true as we look at Brown's study of the supportive kind of discipline it takes to be a successful athlete.

"Athletes not only accept discipline, they embrace it for the benefit of the team," Brown continues, using discipline to "overcome the temptations and pressures and do what is right for their team and themselves at the moment of truth." All truths are parallel!

In our own lives as Christians, Godly discipline can empower us through the Holy Spirit to "overcome the temptations and pressures and do what is right" in our own lives, ultimately producing what is good for us as individuals, for our families, and for our businesses.

Brown shares 5 areas of positive discipline necessary in an athlete's life:

1. The discipline of attentiveness
2. The discipline of enthusiasm being energized
3. The discipline of sportsmanship
4. The discipline of respecting authority
5. The discipline of personal responsibility

When an athlete applies discipline in these 5 areas, "they accomplish more, have a greater sense of

---

16 - Morris Cerullo, "World Evangelism, GVA Financial Breakthrough Spiritual Warfare Bible", 1149

pride, and tend to be better teammates. They are reliable and trustworthy."

Discipline is absolutely necessary to be a successful athlete in the natural realm, and it is absolutely necessary to be a successful Christian in any endeavor you select in both the natural and spiritual realms. Christian discipline empowers us to be able to produce many wonderful results in the targeted areas of our lives!

For God has not given us a spirit of timidity, but of power and love and discipline [sound mind]. 2 Timothy 1:7

That is God's desire for you; not to live a timid life, but to walk boldly in His power, His unconditional love, and in the "sound mind" that comes from the empowerment of Godly discipline for your betterment, growth happiness and prosperity!

Brown goes on in his book to share insights that help the reader distinguish between discipline as a "form of punishment" and discipline that unlocks the exciting results of empowerment:

"For the individual who is not yet an athlete, discipline is normally a dirty word, often associated with a form of punishment. For the non-athlete, this attitude usually results in the person feeling sorry for himself/herself or resisting the intention of discipline. Lack of discipline is often seen in people who choose self-indulgence over self-control."

You see, there is a major difference between viewing discipline as a punishment (sometimes it needs to be) and walking in empowering discipline that allows a person to focus on a challenge or a personal trait for improvement. It takes empowering discipline to redirect your thoughts and actions toward positive attitudes and behavior.

SUCCESS IS NOT NORMALLY LUCK

Most people mistakenly believe that personal or business success usually come from good luck or enormous talent. But, in my humble observations of business owners through the years, most of the successful leaders I know have achieved their accomplishments in a simpler way–through discipline.

Thankfully, discipline has been a key factor in my own individual case of business success. By diligently applying the maxims in Proverbs in my own life, I have been able to develop my skills through the empowerment of biblical discipline, molding and shaping my life, until ultimately I was able to achieve success in my company and in so many of my personal goals. By applying the power of discipline into your own life, Proverbs shares major areas of your life that can grow and improve:

AREA ONE: YOUR PERSONAL GOALS

Often we do not live our lives aware of any plan for the future. We live for the moment, without any consideration of how what we do affects our future. Everything God does has a purpose. Discipline can help you realize that you are responsible for your success (as you dedicate your plans to the Lord), and how long-term persistence really does pay off. Paul understood this process when he wrote (in a message on Minister's Discipline):

In pointing out these things to the brethren, you will be a good servant of Christ Jesus, constantly nourished on the words of the faith and of the sound doctrine which you have been following. 1 Timothy 4:6

Though I only speak briefly about goals in this section, I do have much more to say on the matter. I teach a goals seminar, called Goal Setting For Christians; For speaking engagement inquiries: mikelabahn.com/havemikespeak

AREA TWO: YOUR BUSINESS AND FINANCIAL GOALS

Discipline can make you a better leader and a better manager, help you build a better company and make more money, improve your time-management and problem-solving abilities, and make you more effective and successful at work.

He who neglects discipline despises himself, but he who listens to reproof acquires understanding. Proverbs 15:32

Notice here that Proverbs tells us that the person who neglects empowering discipline "despises himself." Isn't that the definition of a fool? A fool is a person in life who has failed to apply himself in numerous ways, to the point where he doesn't even like himself anymore. The key to biblical success is discipline!

AREA THREE: YOUR OVERALL HAPPINESS

Discipline can help you be happier, healthier, more physically fit, and it can help you in your marriage and your relationships with your children and friends.

Whoever loves discipline loves knowledge, but he who hates reproof is stupid. Proverbs 12:1

Do you see it? Discipline is not something we should shun or hate! Proverbs tells us that the person who "loves discipline" loves knowledge and will become a better person. The other alternative is to just be plain "stupid" (not my words, but His!).

Proverbs challenges us to be more disciplined in every aspect of our lives. Through the biblical guidelines covered in Proverbs you can learn how to be more successful in everything you do - instead of wistfully envying others who you think are just "luckier" than you are. A little biblical discipline can make a major change in your life, so stop making excuses and start applying the maxims in Proverbs!

The fear of the Lord is the beginning of knowledge, but fools despise wisdom and instruction. Proverbs 1:7

PLANNING - AN IMPORTANT ASPECT OF DISCIPLINE

The LORD of hosts has sworn saying, "Surely, just as I have intended so it has happened, and just as I have planned so it will stand" Isaiah 14:24

Everything God did was intentional. The discipline we utilize to plan and set goals allows us to be intentional as well. Nothing will ever change in your life until you determine to make a change, and then write out the plans and set goals to make that change possible. There is an old adage that declares, "If you do not know where you are going, you will probably end up somewhere else."

The mind of a man plans his way, but the LORD directs his steps. Proverbs 16:9

After a plan is set, it then takes Godly, empowering discipline, applied with a right heart rejoicing in the potential for change (rather than complaining about the effort it takes to achieve that change). Going back to our illustration of the athlete, we all envy the superstar who signs a new contract for millions of dollars, but too few are willing to pay the price of scheduling and fulfilling the plans and setting the goals it takes to practice and spend time in the weight room to achieve that fat contract.

Far too many of us Christians claim we want to

change yet consistently refuse to set the plans and goals for change by seeking God and asking Him what areas He wants us to change in our own lives.

As you submit your plans to Him, be open for His modification, guidance and direction. Our plans are futile and doomed to failure unless they line up with God's will for our lives.

Unless the Lord builds the house, they labor in vain who build, unless the Lord guards the city, the watchman keeps awake in vain. Psalm 127:1

Proverbs 19:21 shares this same message:

Many are the plans in a man's heart, but it is the LORD's purpose that prevails.

"Self-help" programs create the illusion that we are in control. We are not. Our gifts and skills are from the Lord, and it is our job to maximize those God-given gifts. Planning is a tool that helps us discern, develop and enrich those God-given gifts.

At the end of each year, my wife, Julie, and I set time apart to seek God as to what plans and goals we should set for ourselves individually and collectively for our marriage, for our family, and for our business for the next year. We make short-term goals (which can be achieved in a year or less), and also establish long term goals (you can go as far as you can see into the future, and then, perhaps a little further). As a result of these planning and goal-setting sessions, and the implementation of the plans God has directed for our lives, we have been able to impact our marriage, our family, and others in significant ways that would never have evolved had we held the attitude, "Well, let's just see what this new year brings."

Write the vision, and make it plain upon tables, that he may run that reads it. Habakkuk 2:2

Our planning sessions cover seven areas in which we make specific goals: career, family, financial, mental, physical, social and spiritual. Together, Julie and I prayerfully seek guidance in these areas, knowing that as we diligently apply the plans God gives to us, they will "surely" lead to "advantage."

The plans of the diligent lead surely to advantage, but everyone who is hasty comes surely to poverty. Proverbs 21:5

As you set your plans and goals, God will honor them, and He will guide you. Even if your goals are not 100 percent of what God wants, He will honor the desires of your heart and direct your steps and your heart in His direction.

All discipline for the moment seems not to be joyful, but sorrowful; yet to those who have been trained by it, afterwards it yields the peaceful fruit of righteousness. Hebrews 12:11

God wants you to experience His "peaceful fruit of righteousness," and you will as you walk through life in the spirit and attitude of Galatians 2:20:

I have been crucified with Christ; and it is no longer I who live [not my plans, but His], *but Christ lives in me; and the life which I now live in the flesh I live by faith in the Son of God, who loved me and gave Himself up for me.*

Chapter 6

GIVING
YOUR WAY TO RICHES

How are you practically honoring God with your finances?

What does it mean to say "my pocketbook is committed to God'"?

How can greed lead to poverty, and generosity to gain?

Why does Proverbs discourage co-signing? List three reasons.

Why is it important scripturally not to mock the poor?

How can consumerism become a hindrance to a Christian life?

Who gave you the health to work? Who gave you the work to do? Who made it possible for you to make money?

Giving tithes and offerings are the basic, fundamental biblical actions we need to follow if we seriously desire to become a financial success in the Christian realm. Matthew 7:24-27 explains the importance of a solid foundation upon which to build our home (family, friends, business, etc.):

Therefore everyone who hears these words of Mine and acts on them, may be compared to a wise man who built his house on the rock. And the rain fell, and the floods came, and the winds blew and slammed against that house; and yet it did not fall, for it had been founded on the rock. Everyone who hears these words of Mine and does not act on them, will be like a foolish man who built his house on the sand. The rain fell, and the floods came, and the winds blew and slammed against that house; and it fell—and great was its fall.

To illustrate the importance of building a biblical, firm financial foundation, I want to share the amazing story of one of my favorite giants for God and His Kingdom!

In a 2007 article that appeared in the Christian Post Reporter, Jennifer Riley wrote about a Christian businessman who was waging his own personal war against poverty by donating all of his company's profits–totaling millions–to help low income people. Hal Taussig owned Untours, a travel agency that provides travelers with a private home as an alternative to staying in a hotel. His company helps "untourists better" learn about the people and cultures they visit.

Besides being a successful businessman, Hal Taussig and his wife, Norma, have given away $5 million in profits over the last two decades to the Untours Foundation which loans money to low-income people trying to start new businesses or improve their lives.

"It wasn't a vow of poverty," said Taussig. "I said I am never going to have any money in the bank... So whatever's left over at the end of the month, I get rid of it."[17] Taussig has not had a car since 1971...he gave his last one away to a hitchhiker. Hal still traveled to the office by bicycle well into his 80's.

Hal and Norma Taussig lived in a modest, "narrow wood-frame" home in Media, PA. The couple skipped the traditional clothes dryer, instead hanging their laundry on a clothesline on the back porch. "I have a mission to fight consumerism," Taussig said. "I think the direction we're [the United States of America] heading in is catastrophic."

The Untours Foundation began five years after the Taussigs founded the Untours business in the mid-1970s. Taussig noticed the rising gap between the rich and poor, which he now believes can only be remedied by economic means.

"My idea is to get capital rather than charity to poor people," he explained. The foundation has made hundreds of loans to small businesses, including one to Home Care Associates of Philadelphia, which provides health care services to patients who want to stay at

---

17 - giantsforgod.com/hal-taussig

home rather than be treated in the hospital. Many of the company's employees were once on welfare. When Taussig gave money to "...Home Care Associates, they doubled their staff that first year, and from that year on they have made a profit. There are 50 people who came off welfare and now get dividends."

The Rev. Maridel Whitmore, Taussig's pastor, said, "You talk about your heart breaking for homeless people and how the church should be outraged about poverty, hunger and war; here's a person doing what we preach. I think he's made us all straighten up a little bit and look at ourselves."

Clearly, Hal Taussig understood and practiced some of the principles Proverbs shares about giving to others and particularly to the poor and needy. In the world's eyes, he may not be considered as wealthy, but he was certainly extremely rich!

In this chapter, I will examine some of the biblical giving principles that can enrich your life, giving it more meaning, as you bless others by practicing and applying them.

GIVING HONORS THE LORD

Honor the LORD from your wealth and from the first of all your produce; so your barns will be filled with plenty and your vats will overflow with new wine. Proverbs 3:9-10

Proverbs tells us that, as Christians, we are to honor God with everything we own—especially our finances. For many of us, there is no greater test of our love for and faith in God than in how we spend our money. To obey the admonition of verse 9 releases the blessings of verse 10. The paradox is that as we are willing to give out of our wealth to honor our God, then we are likely to experience an increase in our own wealth.

We are told to give to Him from our first income, from our first crops, from our first profits; and we are encouraged by the Bible to give to God from our very best – not our leftovers.

You shall bring the choice first fruits of your soil into the house of the LORD your God. Exodus 23:19

Hal Taussig practices this essential truth because he understands that giving honors God, and is foundational to the success of his business. He brings his "choice first fruits" – his company profits – as an offering unto the Lord. This principle of giving our best to God is repeated in many different ways in God's Word.

That you shall take some of the first of all the produce of the ground which you bring in from your land that the LORD your God gives you, and you shall put it in a basket and go to the place where the LORD your God chooses to establish His name. Deuteronomy 26:2

For the businessman/woman, or the wage earner, that "first of all the produce" represents the profits of the business (such as in the case of Untours), or, if you are a wage earner, it represents the first fruit from your paycheck—before you pay anyone else! Some folks believe that principle is fulfilled by the giving of the tithe (giving 10% of your income to God), but I believe that the tithe and the first fruits offering are different. For one thing, the first fruits offering is not limited to 10% and is frequently much more. For another, it is not something "owed" to God but something given out of our own free will. The tithe is expected, an automatic return to God of a 10% portion of what He has given to us. In reality, we owe the tithe to God. However, giving from your first fruits is a voluntary offering that you are not required to give, but you will be blessed by God if you do give it.

"Bring the whole tithe into the storehouse, so that there may be food in My house, and test Me now in this," says the LORD of hosts, "if I will not open for you the windows of heaven and pour out for you a blessing until it overflows." Malachi 3:10

Mr. Taussig decided to give all of the profits from his company to honor God; that amount of profit could easily exceed a 10% tithe. His offering to God is more like an Old Testament first fruits offering than a tithe because he is really giving, not out of a 10% obligation, but based solely upon a desire to bless others from what God brought into his business.

Dr. J. Vernon McGee, a noted Bible teacher, shares this observation:

Don't tell me you are totally committed to the Lord until your pocketbook is committed too. The Lord gives you everything. Some fool may say, 'I have worked hard. I earned this!' But who gave you the health to work? Who gave you the work to do? Who made it possible for you to make money? My friend, God did all of that for you. Acknowledge Him! That is the guideline of total commitment.[18]

Conversely, Newheiser points out that "The one who chooses his own way arrogantly claims that he knows better than God."[19] Many Christians arrogantly declare that they are not going to tithe, or decide to make their own definition of what tithing means. "I give generously to Little League, and that's my tithe to make this world a better place." Such arrogant declarations are destined to bring destruction and ruin into a person's life.

---

18 - McGee, J. Vernon, "Proverbs," 1991, Page 38; Nashville, TN, 37201, Thomas Nelson Publishers.
19 - Newheiser, Jim, "Opening Up Proverbs," Page 60; 2006, Charlotte Hall, MD, 20622, Day One Publishers.

GIVING COMMANDS BLESSINGS BACK TO YOU

So your barns will be filled with plenty and your vats will overflow with new wine. Proverbs 3:10

The biblical principle in this section is that generosity releases God's blessings into your life. Conversely, a tendency towards stinginess can result in becoming poor (which seems contrary to the world's economic logic). Greediness leads to poverty, but generosity enriches in one way or another. As you give to others, your barns (business, family, finances) will begin to burst from God's blessings, and your wine vats (in modern terms, your checking accounts and savings accounts) will brim over. The one who gives will receive far more in return.

The LORD will command the blessing upon you in your barns and in all that you put your hand to, and He will bless you in the land which the LORD your God gives you. Deuteronomy 28:8

Do you see it? The Lord will "command the blessing" upon you. There are not many places I know of in Scripture where God commands a blessing into your life that will cause your vats to overflow in abundance!

Do not fear, O land, rejoice and be glad, for the Lord has done great things. Do not fear, beasts of the field, for the pastures of the wilderness have turned green, for the tree has borne its fruit, the fig tree and the vine have yielded in full. So rejoice, O sons of Zion, and be glad in the Lord your God; for He has given you the early rain for your vindication. And He has poured down for you the rain, the early and latter rain as before. The threshing floors will be full of grain, and the vats will overflow with the new wine and oil. Joel 2:21-24

In God's economy, generosity produces

blessings. Obviously, this teaching is a paradox; the more one gives, the more one receives! In this case, there is actually a biblical self-interest here in that with God's promise of blessing, there is an inherent motivation of increasing one's wealth. Admittedly, that is not the best motivation to give, but nevertheless, it is a biblical maxim that as you give to others, you can generally expect to receive back in return from God's storehouse of inexhaustible wealth.

He who is generous will be blessed, for he gives some of his food to the poor. Proverbs 22:9

Generous hands are blessed hands because they give bread to the poor. One who is gracious to a poor man lends to the LORD, and He will repay him for his good deed. Proverbs 19:17

GIVING INCREASES, WITHHOLDING DECREASES

There is one who scatters, and yet increases all the more, and there is one who withholds what is justly due, and yet it results only in want. The generous man will be prosperous, and he who waters will himself be watered. He who withholds grain, the people will curse him, but blessing will be on the head of him who sells it. Proverbs 11:24-26

God scatters His blessings richly around, and those who have His spirit do the same. The principle here is that generosity, by God's blessing, produces increase, while stinginess leads to poverty instead of the expected gain. The one who gives receives far more in return. Generosity prospers; stinginess impoverishes. This is a biblical principle that is difficult to understand through normal economics. This principle essentially declares that as you are generous, and scatter your wealth to others, somehow, someway, God will flow back more wealth into your life than you gave away so that your net financial report will actually increase. Now that is one for the economists to discuss!

The world of the generous giver grows larger, yet the world of the hoarders, those who are frequently called "stingy," becomes smaller and smaller in God's economy.

The generous man will be prosperous, and he who waters will himself be watered. Proverbs 11:25

The business person or wage earner who blesses others through their financial giving will, in turn, be abundantly blessed. Those who help others will be helped in their time of need.

Honor the LORD from your wealth and from the first of all your produce; so your barns will be filled with plenty and your vats will overflow with new wine. Proverbs 3:9-10

This Scripture provides a succinct summary of what we have learned so far about giving as it is explained in Proverbs:

1   Honor the Lord from your wealth.
2   Give from the first fruits you produce.
3   As you are faithful in 1 & 2, your checking accounts will overflow with new money!

Since Hal Taussig gave over $5 million of his company profits to help better the life of the poor, he clearly understood that the Bible instructs us not to hoard our wealth but to spread it around to others to help improve their lives.

Now this I say, he who sows sparingly will also reap

sparingly, and he who sows bountifully will also reap bountifully. 2 Corinthians 9:6

What I am going to share now is a highly controversial statement, but I believe the truth of this statement is founded in the verses we have studied so far: If you do not have enough money in your checking account, you may not be giving enough!

That is right. If you are giving "sparingly" to others, the Word declares that you will "also reap sparingly." But, if you are giving "bountifully" from your profits and your paycheck, you are guaranteed by God's Word to "reap bountifully."

GIVE AS YOU ARE ABLE

Do not withhold good from those to whom it is due, when it is in your power to do it. Proverbs 3:27

This Scripture advocates that we never walk away from someone who deserves our help ("to whom it is due"); your hand is God's hand for that person. Unfortunately, many Christians cloud this clear mandate with non-biblical thinking, feeling it is justified to borrow without making any repayments. But Psalm 37:21 declares:

The wicked borrows and does not pay back, but the righteous is gracious and gives.

Others violate this biblical maxim by doing everything in their power to evade taxes that they owe, or in keeping back wages due to their employees in direct violation of James 5:4:

Behold, the pay of the laborers who mowed your fields, and which has been withheld by you, cries out against you; and the outcry of those who did the harvesting has reached the ears of the Lord of Sabaoth.

Jeremiah 22:13-17 has extremely harsh words for an employer who does not properly compensate his workers, calling them guilty of practicing "oppression and extortion":

Woe to him who builds his house without righteousness and his upper rooms without justice, who uses his neighbor's services without pay and does not give him his wages, who says, 'I will build myself a roomy house with spacious upper rooms, and cut out its windows, paneling it with cedar and painting it bright red.' "Do you become a king because you are competing in cedar? Did not your father eat and drink and do justice and righteousness? Then it was well with him. "He pled the cause of the afflicted and needy; then it was well. Is not that what it means to know Me?" Declares the Lord. "But your eyes and your heart are intent only upon your own dishonest gain, and on shedding innocent blood and on practicing oppression and extortion.

It actually offends our Creator when we neglect the poor (when we have the ability to help them), because the poor are His children too.

He who oppresses the poor taunts his Maker, but he who is gracious to the needy honors Him. Proverbs 14:31

"Taunts" in the above verse means that a person is actually "mocking, jeering or heckling" the Maker of the Universe. Now, that does not mean that you foolishly give away your money to every Tom, Dick or Harry who stands on a street corner and asks, "Hey, Mister, can you spare $10.00?" (Yes, the price has gone up from the "spare a dime" of a few decades ago.) Note carefully what the verse declares: "to whom it is due." Do not cheat your workers; give the right amount to those you hire: if you have a friend who is working hard, but has fallen on tough times, help them. If someone does an extra good job, then acknowledge that and pay them more. Do these things – if "it is in your power to do it."

Do not say to your neighbor, "Go, and come back, and tomorrow I will give it," when you have it with you. Proverbs 3:28

In other words, do not tell your neighbor "Maybe some other time" or "Try me tomorrow" when you have the money currently available in your pocket to help out someone in need at the moment they need it.

You shall not oppress your neighbor, nor rob him. The wages of a hired man are not to remain with you all night until morning. Leviticus 19:13

A "neighbor" is anyone in need whom God brings across your path or into your life.

CO-SIGNING - A MISUNDERSTOOD ISSUE

Does the challenge to help our neighbor include co-signing for a family member, or a neighbor or friend who needs financial help? Absolutely not!

Proverbs 6:1-5, and many other verses in God's Word, address this hugely misunderstood issue:

My son, if you have become surety for your neighbor, have given a pledge for a stranger, if you have been snared with the words of your mouth, have been caught with the words of your mouth, do this then, my son, and deliver yourself; since you have come into the hand of your neighbor, go, humble yourself, and importune your neighbor. Give no sleep to your eyes, nor slumber to your eyelids; deliver yourself like a gazelle from the hunter's hand and like a bird from the hand of the fowler.

This biblical warning (especially verse 3) literally shouts out, "Don't place yourself at risk in the hands of another! Deliver yourself! Don't co-sign!" Avoid co-signing, it is an unreasonable pledge, a financial entanglement with another over whom you have no power to control.

The Amplified Bible states, "God's Word is very plain on the subject of not underwriting another person's debts."[20]

Proverbs 11:15 declares, *He who is guarantor for a stranger will surely suffer for it, but he who hates being a guarantor is secure.*

How many family relationships have been temporarily crushed or even permanently destroyed as Christians have ignored this biblical principle (or simply did not know about it)? I have heard many a father tell me, "Mike, what could I do? My son needed a new car, and the dealer would not sell it to him without a co-signer." My response is usually something like, "Have him buy a less expensive car for cash." Of course, there are many other options, but never co-signing. I personally know of far too many families where relationships have been destroyed when the family member was unable to repay the loan, and the lenders came against the parents who had co-signed, causing pain to the parents, and in many cases, irreparable damage with the family member unable to pay his/her debt. Proverbs 17:18 calls a person who co-signs for a pledge as one lacking in sense.

A man lacking in sense pledges and becomes guarantor in the presence of his neighbor. Proverbs 17:18

---

20 - Amplified Bible, Large Print Edition, 1987, page 913, Zondervan, Nashville, TN, 37201

Be honest. Do you really have the power to guarantee the actions of another in any area? Of course not. You cannot personally guarantee that another will pay a debt; you are not God, and do not know what the future will bring. That person you pledge for could get fired from their job, laid off, or be afflicted with bad health or a personal injury. All of these circumstances are beyond your control. So, if you are ever asked to co-sign, simply reply, "I cannot help you that way. It is against God's Word. However, there may be some other ways I could help." For example, you could help your son or daughter look for a less expensive car, or save for the car they think they want but do not co-sign for them! Proverbs 22:26 declares the same message in the same strong terms:

Do not be among those who give pledges, among those who become guarantors for debts.

WHEN YOU HONOR THE POOR, YOU HONOR GOD

He who oppresses the poor taunts his Maker, but he who is gracious to the needy honors Him. Proverbs 14:31

This is a Scripture that I suspect Hal Taussig memorized. It clearly says, "You insult your Maker when you exploit the powerless and the poor. However, when you are kind to the poor and help to raise them up out of their poverty, you honor God." The Word shares the same principle in different words in Proverbs 17:5:

He who mocks the poor taunts his Maker; He who rejoices at calamity will not go unpunished.

Imagine if you actually take pleasure in the trials and tribulations of the poor, then you are in line for retribution from your Maker! In His eyes, both poor and rich are equal, and He has made them both:

The rich and the poor have a common bond, the LORD is the maker of them all. Proverbs 22:2

Another major principle here relating to the poor is that the poor, in God's eyes, represent Him!

The King will answer and say to them, "Truly I say to you, to the extent that you did it to one of these brothers of Mine, even the least of them, you did it to Me." Matthew 25:40

If we could really grasp the full significance of that scripture, perhaps all businessmen and wage earners would immediately go out and start their own non-profit foundations to help raise up and better the lives of the poor! Giving to the poor is a little like giving a loan to God, knowing all the while that He is the One who gives the reward to those who are generous in heart to others.

When Hal Taussig showed mercy to the needy and the poor, it was as if he was giving a loan to God, and God always pays back those loans in full. *One who is gracious to a poor man lends to the LORD, and He will repay him for his good deed.* Proverbs 19:17

There are many other Scriptures that share similar points concerning a direct tie-in between honoring the poor and honoring God; there is also a direct tie-in between giving to the poor and God releasing His special blessings into your life. Here are several other verses that share God's heart on this matter.

He who gives to the poor will never want, but he who shuts his eyes will have many curses. Proverbs 28:17

If there is a poor man with you, one of your brothers, in any of your towns in your land which the LORD your God is giving you, you shall not harden your heart, nor close your hand from your poor brother. Deuteronomy 15:7

And whoever in the name of a disciple gives to one of these little ones even a cup of cold water to drink, truly I say to you, he shall not lose his reward. Matthew 10:42

He who shuts his ear to the cry of the poor will also cry himself and not be answered. Proverbs 21:13

If you do not currently consider giving to the poor as one of your spiritual steps to financial freedom, then it is time to re-evaluate your personal perspective and determine how it lines up according to God's Word. Do not plug up your ears to the cries of the poor or your own cries will go unheard and unanswered.

But whoever has the world's goods, and sees his brother in need and closes his heart against him, how does the love of God abide in him? 1 John 3:17

That is a sobering thought: if you see someone in need, and it is within your power to help them and you do not, then God's Word questions whether the love of God really resides in you.

STOP WANTING AND START GIVING

All day long he is craving, while the righteous gives and does not hold back. Proverbs 21:26

Sinners are always wanting what they do not have. The normal, self-centered family strives for the nicest car, the best washer and dryer, the largest and latest flat screen TV, the cellular phone with the most gadgets, bells and whistles; and so on. The God-loyal people like Hal Taussig are always giving what they do have to others. Taussig gave away his car to a hitchhiker and had no craving or need for another. His wife did not covet the latest washer or dryer; a clothes line worked just fine, thank you.

I believe that consumerism is a real and serious blight on America. We are never satisfied and never have enough. Yet, God's Word clearly states here that it is the unrighteous – the sinner – who is "always craving" the next new item to supposedly enhance their life. God's Word instructs us to give and not hold back; it says nothing about a special reward for the American who owns the most self-satisfying toys, electronic gadgets, or the latest and greatest model of a cell phone with the biggest, glare-reducing screen.

When you give to the poor, you are saying "no" to consumerism and "yes" to the blessings of God.

FINALLY, GIVE CHEERFULLY

Now this I say, he who sows sparingly will also reap sparingly, and he who sows bountifully will also reap bountifully. Each one must do just as he has purposed in his heart, not grudgingly or under compulsion, for God loves a cheerful giver. And God is able to make all grace abound to you, so that always having all sufficiency in everything, you may have an abundance for every good deed. 2 Corinthians 9:6-8

When Christians give with a gracious heart, we please God. God cheerfully gives to us, and He loves when His children give in a similar manner. God never gives to us because He has to do it, but because He loves us. We too should strive for hearts that give out of love. From every breath you take, to the house you now live in, to your job and your children, to your ability to hear and see, God has graciously given you all that you have. There is nothing given to you that does not flow from the abundant hand of God.

God is a generous God, and He calls upon us to be generous as well.

Chapter 7

WORKPLACE PROSPERITY
10 VITAL INSTRUCTIONS

How much time, each day, do you spend seeking God's wisdom in His Word? What does your answer tell you about your desire to seek His wisdom?

What foolish sin or hindrance do you now have in your life that you know needs to stop? What is your plan of action to stop it?

Examine yourself, if you have false pride in your life, how can you eliminate it?

If you have a "hot button" that causes you to explode at others, what is it? How can you heal it?

Describe three benefits to operating with a filter on your emotions and your mouth.

What are the dangers of flaunting your knowledge in the workplace?

Are you performing in your workplace up to your God-given potential?

Friend, you cannot make this stuff up.

In our lifetime as we strive to become godly men and women, sometimes we learn from the lessons of others who indulge in actions that the Bible would brand as foolish or even sinful behavior. It is in that vein that I humbly share these real-life little tidbits.

A couple from Cincinnati, Ohio, decided to steal a 55-inch flat screen Hitachi color TV. However, they forgot to take a bigger car for the felony theft. They smashed the front door of a TV and appliance store and greedily grabbed the large TV. As they were driving away from the crime scene, the police stopped them because they noticed that they had a large TV on the back seat of their car, literally hanging out the door as they hurriedly drove home!

Neal sold his car to a 16-year-old teenager for a $150 bag of cocaine. However, he later regretted the decision and cooked up a stupid and foolish story that he was robbed of his car by force. When the police investigated and learned the real circumstances, they arrested Neal for filing a false report (they should have charged him with stupidity, but unfortunately stupidity is not against the law!), and then arrested the teenager for selling drugs.

A man who was hit by a car in New York City got up uninjured, but he laid back down in front of the car when a bystander told him to pretend he was hurt so he could collect insurance money. The car then accidentally rolled forward down the hill and crushed him to death.

Hitting on the novel idea that he could end his wife's incessant nagging by giving her a good scare, a man fashioned an elaborate harness to make it look as though he had hanged himself. When his wife came home and saw him, she fainted. Hearing a disturbance, a neighbor came over and, finding what she thought were two corpses, seized the opportunity to loot the place. As she was leaving the room, her arms laden with stolen goods, the outraged and suspended man kicked her stoutly in the backside. This so surprised the lady that she dropped dead of a heart attack. The man was acquitted of manslaughter; later, he and his wife were reconciled.

Bill was filming a public service announcement on "The Dangers of Low-Level Bridges" when the truck he was standing on passed under a low level bridge killing him.

Surprised while burglarizing a house, a thief fled out the back door, climbed over a nine-foot wall, dropped down, and found himself in the city prison yard! Friend, you cannot make this stuff up.

There are many biblical lessons we can learn from these and thousands of other incidents in life that we experience or witness every year. In this chapter, I would like to share ten Scriptural conclusions on how to avoid being foolish or stupid in the daily affairs of work and business and how to walk instead in biblical wisdom.

1 - LISTEN TO INSTRUCTION

The fear of the LORD is the beginning of knowledge;

fools despise wisdom and instruction. Proverbs 1:7

When Bill was working as an employee, filming his public service announcement, the first thing he should have done was seek the wisdom and instruction from the State Transportation Department as to the height of bridges in the route he would be traveling under as he stood on the truck (a dangerous idea in and of itself).

Of course, the primary wisdom and instruction we all need to heed comes from God. To do that, we need to humble ourselves, bow down to Him, and respect the knowledge and wisdom in His Word. Only a fool would ignore His instruction manual for living. For example, stealing from work and believing you can get away with it is about as stupid as that man standing up in a traveling truck.

How do you begin to obtain His wisdom and knowledge? By reverencing the wisdom in His Word. In Scripture, the "Fear of the Lord" means to reverence and respect what it declares.

And to man He said, 'Behold, the fear of the Lord, that is wisdom; and to depart from evil is understanding. Job 28:28

Ecclesiastes 12:13 summarizes this concept extremely well: *The conclusion, when all has been heard, is: fear God and keep His commandments, because this applies to every person.*

2 - AVOID SIMPLE-MINDED APPROACHES TO LIFE

If you are uncertain precisely what being simple minded means, that is probably a good thing. You can count on one thing: having a simple-minded employee is not a good thing to an employer.

The neighbor who thought there were two corpses next door was both simple-minded and foolishly sinful. She was simple-minded to mistakenly believe that a few trinkets, stolen from her dead neighbors' home, were somehow worth the risk of jail; she was foolishly sinful to think that robbing dead people was somehow less offensive than robbing the living.

How long, O naive ones, will you love being simple-minded? And scoffers delight themselves in scoffing and fools hate knowledge? Proverbs 1:22

One of the pastors of our church, delivering the end of his sermon in obvious frustration, asked the congregation: "How long will we continue falling into the same foolish, sinful traps such as pornography on the internet? How long will we wallow in the ignorance that the world has anything materially to offer us? How long will we refuse to learn the lessons from God's Word?"

My pastor was obviously a bit frustrated because day after day, year after year, he meets with businessmen who somehow believe that by cheating they could succeed. He meets with spouses who somehow believe that their affair are just what they needed to make it through life. Solomon fittingly pleads with God in Proverbs 1:4:

To give prudence to the naive, to the youth knowledge and discretion.

Those who have disciplined themselves to not act from spontaneous emotions will generally do well in life. Others react like the neighbor lady, spontaneously doing a foolish thing without any serious thought of the consequences. Proverbs 22:3 says, *The prudent sees the evil and hides himself, but the naive go on, and are punished for it.* In this neighbor lady's case, her unexpected punishment was that she ended up being a victim of a heart attack.

3 - GIVE GRACE TO OTHERS

Grace giving is an important part of not being a fool. *Though He scoffs at the scoffers, yet He gives grace to the afflicted* Proverbs 3:34. This Scripture is a bit confusing, but here is what I personally believe it means: A wise man knows enough not to value or heed the ridicule and scoffing of others. In essence, he gives their words and warnings a cold shoulder because he perceives them as proud skeptics. However, if you are down on your luck, that same wise man is right there to give you grace and to help you out. The moral? If you are a grace-giver to others, such as your employees or your employer, then God will give you grace in return! But He gives a greater grace; therefore it says, *God is opposed to the proud, but gives grace to the humble.* James 4:6

How can you be a good worker if you are so proud and arrogant that you do not take correction? How can you be a good boss if you are too proud to listen to input from your employees?

Important note: As a boss or manager, when you have the need to correct an employee, you should approach the situation with the mindset that this will be a constructive conversation and not a stern lecture.

Another Scripture addresses the same truth to younger men who, in their youth, tend to gravitate towards a know-it-all attitude, and a huge dose of false pride. These know-it-alls in the workplace are normally so insecure that anything remotely resembling a correction is viewed defensively as a threat to their competence. "Don't you dare tell me how to do that job. Who do you think you are?"

You younger men, likewise, be subject to your elders; and all of you, clothe yourselves with humility toward one another, for God is opposed to the proud, but gives grace to the humble. 1 Peter 5:5

If you are under the supervision of an elder, listen and learn. When was the last time you met a respectful, humble young man? If you know one, treasure that friendship. If you are an employer, hire him!

4 - THINK BEFORE YOU SPEAK OR ACT

As our friendly burglar learned, the next time you jump over a fence, make sure that it does not have a nine foot drop behind it that puts you into a prison yard. To prosper, it is imperative that we learn to monitor both our words and our actions, and not leap or act before we think.

The wise will inherit honor, but fools display dishonor. Proverbs 3:35

If you are wise enough to monitor your words and actions in your work environment, you will be rewarded with honor – and probably a promotion. However, if you want to major in stupid thinking and careless actions, you will receive dishonor and the booby prizes of life – and you will probably be fired, or your business will fail.

The wise of heart will receive commands, but a babbling fool will be ruined. Proverbs 10:8

At my company I have unfortunately seen too

many fools through the years: a wise worker will take orders with humility and grace; a fool with an empty head will come unglued whenever asked to do something he does not agree with, does not understand, or feels is somehow a criticism. If this keeps happening at your company, face this fact: a fool with an empty head seldom changes. You cannot expect that foolish worker to ever be receptive to your instruction; you just need to fire the rebel and move on to someone who has acquired the wisdom to receive correction or instructions with the right heart.

Do not reprove a scoffer, or he will hate you, reprove a wise man and he will love you. Proverbs 9:8

Employers or supervisors, stop wasting so much time and energy during the day trying to correct the one person who refuses correction! Jesus understood that there were even going to be scoffers of His Words. That is why he declared,

"Therefore everyone who hears these words of Mine and acts on them, may be compared to a wise man who built his house on the rock." Matthew 7:24

If you are a boss or a supervisor, be thankful for the wise men and women in your life who listen to your corrections. Treasure them, promote them and build your company around them.

5 - AVOID SLANDER, DECEIT, AND OFFICE GOSSIP

He who conceals hatred has lying lips, and he who spreads slander is a fool. Proverbs 10:18

Liars secretly hoard hatred in their hearts, but fools openly spread slander. When Neal sold his car for drugs, and then filed the false police report, he openly and foolishly spread slander against the car buyer, and that came back to reap justice on his life. So many of us think we can say things against a co-worker or an employee without any repercussions or consequences. That simply is not the way the world works.

Recently, a famous sports personality received an $11 million judgment against him and his employer, Madison Square Garden, because he slandered a female co-worker by calling her inappropriate names. Much of his well-earned professional sports reputation, fashioned over a long decade of hard work as a professional basketball player, was tarnished, if not undone, by a few stupid words carelessly spoken in the work environment.

The lips of the righteous feed many, but fools die for lack of understanding. Proverbs 10:21

The Bible speaks of a sport that none of us want to excel in. Proverbs 10:23 says, *Doing wickedness is like sport to a fool, and so is wisdom to a man of understanding.* Longman puts it another way: "The idea is that doing evil is something that fools actually relish [like a sport], not something that circumstances force upon them."[21]

A fool shows his annoyance at once, but a prudent man overlooks an insult. Proverbs 12:16

Proverbs values self-control and repression over an impulsive display of rash emotion, just as Proverbs also values silence over too much talk. Clearly, there is a major benefit to operating with a filter on our emotions and upon our words. An empty-headed person mistakenly believes that mischief and degrading words are fun, but a mindful person relishes wisdom and monitors his tongue.

He who speaks truth tells what is right, but a false

---

21 - Longman III, Tremper, "Proverbs," 2007, Page 240; Grand Rapids, MI, Baker Academic.

witness, deceit. Proverbs 12:17

Truthful witness by a good person clears the air, but liars lay down a smoke screen of deceit.

6 - CONTROL YOUR TEMPER AND YOUR TONGUE

A fool's anger is known at once, but a prudent man conceals dishonor. Proverbs 12:16

Fools have short fuses and explode all too quickly in the workplace; the prudent quietly shrug off insults. Sir Walter Raleigh, a man of known courage and honor, was once verbally assaulted by a hot-headed, rash youth, who proceeded to challenge him, and, on his refusal to argue, spit in his face in public. Sir Walter took out his handkerchief to wipe his face, and with great calmness, made this reply:

"Young man, if I could as easily wipe your blood from my conscience as I can this injury from my face, I would this moment take away your life."[22] The youth, with a strong sense of his improper behavior, fell on his knees, and begged forgiveness.

I know of a few companies where the boss or his wife simply refuse to control their tempers around their employees. Clearly, although fools may not listen well, they certainly feel the freedom to talk far more than they should. The employee turnover at those companies is constant because the employees quickly spot the pattern of anger and just about as quickly decide that it does not make for a good work environment—so they move on to a more peaceful situation.

Conversely, I have had employees at my company who have lost their tempers with clients, and it was my responsibility, once a pattern was discerned, to help them move on before my company name and

---

22 - Dodd, Williams, "Sermons To Young Men", 1792, Page 343

reputation were permanently damaged.

A fool always loses his temper, but a wise man holds it back. Proverbs 29:11

The wicked person expends his anger suddenly, quickly and without any filters...all at once. But the wise person dispenses his displeasure gradually, not in the heat of his anger. He waits with deliberation and then releases his displeasure slowly and in moderation.

7 - DON'T FLAUNT YOUR KNOWLEDGE

A prudent man conceals knowledge, but the heart of fools proclaims folly. Proverbs 12:23

Prudent people in the workplace do not flaunt their knowledge; instead, they share it without a sense of superiority, but with a sense of constructive instruction. The most misleading way to feel wise is to feel superior. Talkative fools, on the other hand, broadcast their silliness to anyone who will listen. Proverbs 10:14 tells us, *"Wise men store up knowledge, but with the mouth of the foolish, ruin is at hand."*

Every prudent man acts with knowledge, but a fool displays folly. Proverbs 13:16

When you are in the workplace, it is important that you use the knowledge that God has given you for the betterment of your company. Never use it to embarrass others, or to flaunt what you know. Perhaps this is best summed up in Proverbs 15:2:

The tongue of the wise makes knowledge acceptable, but the mouth of fools spouts folly.

A common-sense person lives with a biblical

sense for work and life; a fool litters the workplace with silliness. The biblical sense includes the repression of anger in the workplace in order to help maintain and retain relationships.

8 - DILIGENCE, DISCIPLINE AND GOOD RESULTS

The hand of the diligent will rule, but the slack hand will be put to forced labor. Proverbs 12:24

Diligent workers will ultimately find positive results from their perseverance; they will enjoy the freedom and peace of mind in the workplace that comes from a job well done. However, the lazy, and those who simply do not take the time to perform their jobs at an acceptable level are oppressed by work, and grow to hate their jobs. They never will experience the sense of freedom and job satisfaction that the diligent worker enjoys. Bill Hybels, a noted scholar of Proverbs, shared this basic biblical maxim for worker success:

"Here's the question, Are you "working with all your heart" at your place of employment, at home or at school? I am not asking if you are expending the necessary energy to do the tasks assigned to you. "I am asking if you are doing every project that comes your way to the best of your God-given potential?"[23]

Notice the fate of the lazy: "forced labor," which, when you think about it, is really the hardest work of all. Ironic, isn't it? Those who try and avoid work the most will ultimately end up doing the hardest work of all because forced labor is the only thing they can be trusted doing.

Bill Hybel, in the same book just cited, wrote this insightful truth about discipline as a key element to our success in life:

---

[23] - Hybels, Bill, "Making Life Work," Page 42; 1998, Downers Grove, IL, 60515, Inter Varsity Press.

"When it comes to the work of living, Proverbs tells us that the most indispensable tool available to all of us is discipline. Without it we cannot live productive, satisfying lives. Proverbs 13:8 says, *He who ignores discipline comes to poverty and shame.* While poverty and shame may manifest themselves in many forms, ignoring discipline always manifests itself in a life sliding toward ruin. If we fail to take discipline seriously, we do so at our own peril."

Over and over again, Proverbs emphasizes the need to set up a plan, and then have the discipline (diligence) to bring that plan into fruition.

The plans of the diligent lead surely to advantage, but everyone who is hasty comes surely to poverty. Proverbs 21:5

9 - SURROUND YOURSELF WITH CAPABLE PEOPLE

Leave the presence of a fool, or you will not discern words of knowledge. Proverbs 14:7

Fools are a waste of your time, and will bring your workplace to ruination. Escape quickly from the company of fools; they are a drain of your time and words. As Proverbs 23:9 declares:

Do not speak in the hearing of a fool, for he will despise the wisdom of your words.

The wisdom of the sensible is to understand his way, but the foolishness of fools is deceit. Proverbs 14:8

Clearly, the wisdom of the wise will help keep your business on track and doing well, while the stupidity and poor judgment of fools will only land your company into bankruptcy.

Chapter 8

FOOLS, FOLLY & FRIVOLITY

List at least three characteristics that constitute a person you would call a fool. Do you possess any of those traits?

Name some biblical values that you need to incorporate into your daily life, and describe how you are going to do it.

An extremely defensive employee normally signals what kind of internal problems for the workplace?

In some detail, write how you believe your current employer views your performance.

Why is it biblically important to be honest with your employer concerning your work accountability?

What type of problems can a fool cause in the workplace?

Explain what "To spring to the defense of one's honor is to do it a disservice," means to you.

Why are pride and arrogance deterrents to being an effective employee?

Wisdom is free, but it is also optional.

LeLand Gregory, in his book, *Idiots at Work: Chronicles of Workplace Stupidity*, delightfully reveals how the workplace is "packed with the dumb, dumber, and dumbest humans on the face of the planet." Consider these 3 amazing examples:

A woman sued Eastman Kodak to improve the lighting conditions on her job. She worked in a darkroom!

The Ontario Federation of Labor installed a "bad boss" hotline to try and compile a better understanding of labor problems - only to have the system crash soon after startup because they had too many calls!

A woman went to an interview while listening to a Walkman, explaining, "I can listen to you [the interviewer] and to my music at the same time."

The truth is, none of us have to search very far to find a fool in the workplace; unfortunately, fools are only too anxious to share their antics with the rest of us. There are a couple of key characteristics about a fool:

Fools do not learn from their mistakes, they are normally full of their own "wisdom," and fools are not open to input from others.

These characteristics give us a test, an extended

picture of what it looks like to be a fool. Such a person is unreliable, unteachable, and amazingly, they are also arrogant. In turn, the fool is likely to be a sluggard (Proverbs 12:13-16), a busybody (Proverbs 26:17-22), and a liar (Proverbs 26:23-28).

We have all experienced moronic managers, office idiots, stupid shareholders, daft decision makers, poor planners, and outstanding examples of cubical klutzes. Here are a few more examples of business blunders:

A woman purchased several items from a department store and was handed the credit card receipt to sign. The cashier noticed that the back of the woman's credit card was not signed and told her that she could not complete the transaction without a signed card. The woman complied and signed the back of the card immediately after signing her receipt. The cashier took both the receipt and the card, held them up, and compared the signatures. They matched!

An article in the Employee Relations Law Journal explains, "Many individuals who become violent toward customers or coworkers suffer from some form of mental disorder. Yet, for an employer to be too careful in screening potentially dangerous persons out of the work force is to invite liability for discrimination under the ADA (Americans With Disabilities Act), while to be not careful enough is to invite tragedy and horrendous liability for negligent hire or negligent retention." Did you get that?

As you read the biblical warnings and admonitions in this chapter concerning fools, ineffective communicators, those manifesting stupidity, and hot-tempered workers, they will hopefully provide you with the principles and guidelines you need to spot and eliminate them within your own workplace or business environment. One of my favorite stories concerning stupidity comes from the venerable J. Vernon McGee:

"A man driving down the highway had a flat tire, so he pulled over to the side of the road. It happened he was parked by an insane asylum, and one of the men from the asylum was on the other side of the fence. He was watching the man as he changed the tire. He didn't say anything, just stood there and watched. As the man took off the wheel of the car, he placed all the nuts that he had taken off into the hubcap. Then he accidentally tilted the hubcap so all the nuts fell out and went into a sewer, and he couldn't retrieve them. He stood there scratching his head, wondering what in the world he would do. The man behind the fence who had been watching him said, 'Why don't you take a nut off each of the other wheels and put them on this wheel? You could drive safely down to the filling station and there you can buy nuts so that you can fix your wheel.' The man looked at him in amazement. 'Why didn't I think of that?' he asked. 'You are in the institution, I am out, and yet you are the one who thought of it.' The onlooker answered, 'I may be crazy, but I'm not stupid!' Well, this book of proverbs is attempting to get you and me out of a position of being stupid in life today. I think we shall find it to be a great help to us. This book has quite a bit to say about stupidity as we shall see."[24]

Proverbs contains many biblical nuggets to help you avoid stupidity and to alert you on how to spot a fool; other verses instruct you on how to deal with a fool once you spot him/her.

FOOLS MOCK SIN

Fools mock at sin, but among the upright there is good will. Proverbs 14:9

---

[24] - McGee, J. Vernon, "Proverbs," 1991, Pages 20-21; Nashville, TN, 37201, Thomas Nelson Publishers.

Probably the quickest way to spot a fool is that they have absolutely no respect for God's Word, nor for the mandates of God's instructions or commandments. Wise people see and can spot the approach of sin in their lives, and quickly remove themselves from it, while fools wade right into sin and then suffer the consequences. In the workplace, a fool is quick to sin – steal, cuss, fornicate, lie, cheat – and is slow to be corrected.

Just as a fool is a destructive influence in the workplace, conversely, those who lead an "upright" life, a moral life, a godly life, will bring good will into their offices. The Bible tells us in Proverbs 11:20 that:

The perverse in heart are an abomination to the LORD, but the blameless in their walk are His delight.

Men and women with godly values are appreciated and valued in the workplace. Men and women who are honest, manifest integrity, have a sense of fairness, and a firm commitment to their word are those who are admired, respected and promoted by their bosses or their clients (clients promote you by bringing you their repeat business).

FOOLS REJECT CORRECTION

A fool rejects his father's discipline, but he who regards reproof is sensible. Proverbs 15:5

This principle ties in rather closely with the first: fools mock sin. Clearly, if a fool rejects his father's discipline (the correction of elders), he will also reject authority in the workplace, and will ultimately reject the prime authority – Almighty God and His Word. Moral dropouts will never listen to their immediate supervisors, nor welcome correction within the workplace.

Fools will reject even the wisest advice, often responding to the wise advice with hostility instead of appreciation for the information. Fools routinely reject wisdom, especially if that wisdom involves any sort of criticism of their personal or workplace behavior. One of my favorite verses for the counseling of business leaders and work supervisors comes from Matthew 7:6:

Do not give what is holy to dogs, and do not throw your pearls before swine, or they will trample them under their feet, and turn and tear you to pieces.

When you encounter a defensive employee who constantly tries to justify his actions when corrected, move on to a new employee. Fools simply refuse to listen. *Do not speak in the hearing of a fool, for he will despise the wisdom of your words* Proverbs 23:9. There is a saying that goes, "Hire slow, fire fast." This workplace maxim is normally practiced in reverse. In the case of a defensive employee, the workplace will greatly improve when the boss learns to fire the fool fast.

Bill Hybels observed that the word "fool," in today's world implies a person with low intelligence. However, in biblical times, fools could have a high intelligence quota, and even a reputation for success. In the Bible, a fool is a person that ignores "God's wisdom, preferring to follow the shifting dictates of the crowd or their own fallible opinions."[25] Fools are often intelligent enough to beat the system in one manner or another, yet their cleverness can frequently lead to their ruin.

If you have employees who poke fun at your instructions behind your back, fire them because they will undermine your authority. If you are an employee who openly mocks your boss, Scripture calls you a fool. Stop what you are doing and start becoming an asset to your company. If you are a supervisor, do not waste your time with those who always want to argue with

---

25 - Hybels, Bill, "Making Life Work," Page 20; 1998, Downers Grove, IL, 60515, Inter Varsity Press.

you; it is probably time they move on to another place, because only *The fear of the LORD is the beginning of knowledge; fools despise wisdom and instruction.* Proverbs 1:7

FOOLS MANIFEST UNPLEASANT TRAITS EASILY

Excellent speech is not fitting for a fool, much less are lying lips to a prince. Proverbs 17:7

In the workplace, do not ever expect to hear eloquence or wisdom coming out of the mouth of a fool. If anything, because they do not respect or study the Word of God, you can expect them to speak nonsense, lies and worldly thoughts rather than the real wisdom that comes from someone bathed in God's Word.

Wisdom is too exalted for a fool, he does not open his mouth in the gate. Proverbs 24:7

Clearly the fool of Proverbs is not necessarily the person who is unintelligent. The fool is someone who has rejected the counsel of wisdom and whose understanding of life is fundamentally wrong. The fool of Proverbs is generally arrogant, scheming and lacking sadly in any form of self-control. To clarify what proverbs thinks of a fool, Jim Newheiser, in his book Opening Up Proverbs, compiled this interesting list of characteristics (or more precisely, defects) that make up a fool:

1. He is a flatterer and a manipulator (Proverbs 26:6)
2. He is lazy (Proverbs 10:4-22)
3. He is a liar (Proverbs 12:22; 26:18-28)
4. He is a thief (Proverbs 28:24)
5. He is unwise with money (Proverbs 14:24; 28:24)
6. He is immoral (Proverbs 7:22; 29:3)
7. He uses intoxicating substances Proverbs 23:29-35

8   He is a glutton Proverbs 28:7 [26]

In the same book, Jim offers definitions of the "naïve," the "fool," and the "scoffer." He defines them as follows:

"The naïve is committed neither to good nor evil...Because he has not devoted himself to wisdom, he is vulnerable to seduction...Because he has not yet given himself over to folly, there is hope that he will turn to wisdom before it is too late.

The fool (Hebrew *keciyl*) has rejected wisdom and has become morally insensitive. He is so occupied with the things of the world and the things of God are of no concern to him... A stronger word for fool (Hebrew *eviyl*) is used in Proverbs 1:7. This man loves folly and despises wisdom and instruction."

The scoffer is the free thinking cynic who mocks at God, sin and judgment. He is hardened against any reproof."[27]

Lying lips are an abomination to the LORD, but those who deal faithfully are His delight. Proverbs 12:22

To those of you who mistakenly believe you can somehow please your employer by feeding him/her untruths, instead of making yourself accountable for both the good things you do, and your mistakes, you are definitely a candidate for fool status!

FOOLS NEVER MANIFEST WISDOM

Why is there a price in the hand of a fool to buy wisdom, when he has no sense? Proverbs 17:16

If a vendor could sell wisdom in the local

---

26 - Newheiser, Jim, "Opening Up Proverbs," Page 150; 2006, Charlotte Hall, MD, 20622, Day One Publishers.
27 - Newheiser, Jim, "Opening Up Proverbs," Page 39; 2006, Charlotte Hall, MD, 20622, Day One Publishers.

shopping mall, it is clear from this Scripture that you would never find a fool ready to buy the vendor's goods. In truth, a fool would probably not even recognize wisdom if it sat "for sale" on a store shelf at a wonderful discount. Wealth can never buy wisdom for a fool who does not choose to love it.

On the other hand, a wise person can arrive at truth (without money) with a humble heart and a desire to seek truth in God's Word. Wisdom cannot be purchased as a commodity, but needs to be earned through humility, diligence, perseverance, and an open mind – commodities not frequently found in a foolish worker. Wisdom can also be accumulated by the methodical and daily study of God's Word. In my observation, wisdom is free, but it is also optional. If one determines to read and apply the Bible, and in particular the Book of Proverbs, one would have all the wisdom one needs to lead a successful life. Wisdom is something that all in business should strive for, but understand, the only way to purchase it is through the virtues we have discussed here.

Buy truth, and do not sell it, get wisdom and instruction and understanding. Proverbs 23:23

The word "instruction" appears 26 times in Proverbs, so it obviously is one of the more important aspects of this amazing book. It is vital that we receive the words written in Proverbs as instruction for our lives if we want to walk in peace, prosperity and happiness.

FOOLS BRING PARENTS (AND BOSSES) SORROW

He who sires a fool does so to his sorrow, and the father of a fool has no joy. Proverbs 17:21

This proverb is a clear illustration of the

circumstantial nature of the proverbial truth. It assumes that the parents are wise themselves. If they are wise, then having a fool for a child brings misery and sorrow to the parents; clearly, it is not fun being the parent of one who refuses instruction or behaves in a rebellious manner.

A wise son makes a father glad, but a foolish son is a grief to his mother. Proverbs 10:1

The same parental principle applies in the workplace. Your boss or your clients essentially become your new authority figures, constantly giving you instructions, expecting you to be humble enough and submissive enough to receive those instructions without any sign of rebellion, and follow them through to a satisfactory completion that pleases the client.

Two other Scriptures back up this single concept. As you read these words of wisdom, where it says "father" substitute the phrase "authority figure" – the person who gives you instruction or who supervises your work performance. Where it says "son" substitute the word "employee."

A self-confident and foolish son is a grief to his father and bitterness to her who bore him. Proverbs 17:25 AMP

A foolish son is destruction to his father, and the contentions of a wife are a constant dripping. Proverbs 19:13 AMP

These verses suggest that fools are only interested in their own desires, and do not have the patience to achieve the goals associated with wisdom, nor do they listen to people with competence.

FOOLS SPEAK WITHOUT THINKING

A fool does not delight in understanding, but only in revealing his own mind. Proverbs 18:2

Fools care nothing for thoughtful discourse; all they do is run off at the mouth, revealing the lack of depth in their own minds. Dr. J. Vernon McGee once said, "If I stop to think before I speak, I won't have to worry afterwards about what I said before."[28] You can always recognize a fool in the workplace – he is the one constantly talking without saying anything of value; a fool releases frivolous words of folly.

A prudent man conceals knowledge, but the heart of fools proclaims folly. Proverbs 12:23

Because fools speak without thinking, it is frivolous to try and answer a fool. *Do not answer a fool according to his folly, or you will also be like him* Proverbs 26:4. Do not dignify or respond to the stupidity of a fool, or you will only look foolish yourself. Proverbs 23:9 warns:

Do not speak in the hearing of a fool, for he will despise the wisdom of your words.

Should you feel it is your noble, Christian duty to change or reform a fool, take a few minutes to meditate upon these wise words from Proverbs 29:9: *When a wise man has a controversy with a foolish man, the foolish man either rages or laughs, and there is no rest*. In your attempts in the reformation process, you will likely be met with either rage or laughs. Not exactly productive results.

Instead, *Answer a fool as his folly deserves, that he not be wise in his own eyes* Proverbs 26:5. In other words, answer a fool in simple terms so he does not

---

28 - McGee, J. Vernon, "Proverbs," 1991, Pages 15, 20-21, 38, 108, 139, 157, 172, 198, 234, 240; Nashville, TN, 37201, Thomas Nelson Publishers.

mistakenly believe he is smart and start to get a swelled head.

Here is the plain truth: a fool and his ways are difficult to change. *Though you pound a fool in a mortar with a pestle along with crushed grain, yet his foolishness will not depart from him,* Proverbs 27:22. In essence, this verse says, "You can pound on a fool all you like, but you are not very likely to pound out their foolishness, no matter how hard you try to change him."

I can just hear some reader thinking, "I was a fool once, and somebody took the time to set me straight." Yes, change does happen – but in the right timing. When a person is a fool, it means that person is in a season (hopefully short) in his/her life when sin is rampant, when they are not responding to correction, and they are rejecting those in authority on a course to self-destruction. When the person decides to abandon that sinful lifestyle, then correction and change are possible.

FOOLS CAUSE STRIFE

A fool's lips bring strife, and his mouth calls for blows. Proverbs 18:6

Allowing strife to exist is one of the quickest ways to sabotage your business, workplace or home. Have you ever experienced someone in your office who constantly stirs up trouble and strife? The Bible calls that person a fool! The words of a fool start fights, cause negative vibrations in the office, and distract workers from their assigned tasks. *Keeping away from strife is an honor for a man, but any fool will quarrel.* Proverbs 20:3

Dr. J. Vernon McGee offers this bit of wisdom:

"One of the marks of a Christian should be that he does not prolong tension and strife. Someone has said that the only persons we should try to 'get even' with are the people who have helped us. In other words, repay good with good, but don't try to 'get even' with your enemies.

"A fool can cause an entire office staff to lose focus on their assignments. And yet, from my experience, that loudmouth gets a huge percentage of the staff's attention as they try to placate and appease the loudest voice. In colloquial terms, the world says, 'The squeaky wheel gets the grease.'"[29]

In the book of Proverbs, it frequently advocates conflict avoidance. Clearly, a wise person with humility often has the good judgment to ignore some offenses in order to prevent needless conflict, while the prideful fool does not hesitate to enter into arguments and conflicts. It has been said that "To spring to the defense of one's honor is to do it a disservice."

My straightforward recommendation? If you cannot gag that fool, or convince that person to hold their tongue then fire him/her, and your office will dramatically jump in productivity. As Scripture declares:

A fool's mouth is his ruin, and his lips are the snare of his soul. Proverbs 18:7

Fools are undone and identified by their unchecked, diarrhea mouths that never stop running. Their very souls and spirits, and, unfortunately, the souls and spirits of those around them are susceptible to being crushed by an avalanche of negative, empty, destructive, worthless words.

---

29 - McGee, J. Vernon, "Proverbs," 1991, Page 172; Nashville, TN, 37201, Thomas Nelson Publishers.

Wise men store up knowledge, but with the mouth of the foolish, ruin is at hand. Proverbs 10:14

To survive and prosper, a businessman/woman or supervisor needs productive people who know when to volunteer information, and when to remain quiet, keeping certain confidential company information to themselves. Proverbs 13:3 declares:

The one who guards his mouth preserves his life; the one who opens wide his lips comes to ruin.

A FOOL VALUES WEALTH & STATUS ABOVE INTEGRITY

Often, God's ways do not coincide with how the world thinks or acts. I cannot think of any area where God and the world are more apart from each other than in the area of money.

Better is the poor who walks in his integrity than he who is crooked though he be rich. Proverbs 28:6

Do you see it? According to God, it is far better to walk in integrity than in ill-gotten wealth. It is far better to be a poor man who walks in God's biblical precepts than to be a person who is perverse in speech, who is not trustworthy, who is quick to cheat, and who has only one goal: the accumulation of wealth – no matter what it takes.

Many different Proverbs state, in one way or another, the truth contained in 14:2:

He who walks in his uprightness fears the LORD, but he who is devious in his ways despises Him.

I hope that those of you who are reading this book will never despise the Lord, but declare and live your lives according to Psalm 26:11, praying to the Lord:

But as for me, I shall walk in my integrity; redeem me, and be gracious to me.

FOOLS OFTEN SEE THEMSELVES AS WISE

Do you see a man wise in his own eyes? There is more hope for a fool than for him. Proverbs 26:12

Being a proud person who is "wise in his own eyes" is bad enough, but it is even more repulsive when that person is completely unaware of his own ignorance, functioning in total deception concerning his real lack of wisdom, and his need for the counsel of others. One of the vices that frequently comes with success is pride—successful people in business tend to think they are smart, and that they are something special. My pastor, Mark Hoffman, pointed out in one of his sermons that one of the challenges for a successful businessman is to stay humble enough to listen to others.[30]

Proverbs 3:7 warns, *Do not be wise in your own eyes; fear the LORD and turn away from evil.*

Of course, there are degrees of foolishness, with intellectual conceit being perhaps the most stupid and the most difficult to remedy. Charles Bridges once wrote this simple prayer to help him resist intellectual conceit:

"Lord, preserve me from this hopeless delusion. Pull down all my pride and imagined wisdom. Take the blindness from my eyes that I may know what I am in Your sight. Clothe me with humility from the sole of my foot to my heart." [31]

A FOOL IS QUICK TO ANGER

A fool always loses his temper, but a wise man holds it back. Proverbs 29:11

---

[30] - Hoffman, Mark, "Overcoming this Present Crisis," 2009, Foothills Christian Church message.
[31] - Bridges, Charles, "An Exposition On the Book of Proverbs," 1847, Pg 419; Carlisle, PA, 17013, Banner of Truth Publications.

The expression "hothead" is reserved for those in the workplace who cannot control their tempers. They are demonstrating, through their rants and ravings, an inability to control their temper. A wise man will have an unexpected, unpleasant event happen and reserve his reactions until he quietly mulls over his calculated response. He overcomes his anger with humility, then determines an orderly response to the issue (which could be no response at all...simply overlooking the offense). *A fool's anger is known at once, but a prudent man conceals dishonor.* Proverbs 12:16

STUPIDITY - ACCORDING TO PROVERBS

Why does a pizza get to your house faster than an ambulance? Why are there handicap parking places in front of a skating rink? Why do drugstores make the sick walk all the way to the back of the store to get their prescriptions while healthy people can buy cigarettes at the front? Why do people order double cheeseburgers, large fries, and a diet coke? Why do banks leave their doors open and then chain the pens to the counters? We use the word "politics" to describe the process so well: "Poli" in Latin means "many" and "tics" means "bloodsucking creatures."

Despite the humor listed here, the words "stupidity" and "stupid" are not normally politically correct in today's world. If I called an employee "stupid" I would likely be called up on charges of verbal abuse before the State Labor Board. Calling someone stupid can imply, in today's world, that a person is mentally handicapped, and people with a low level of intelligence do not have any choice in the matter and should never be mocked or be ridiculed in any way!

The definition of stupid in today's world is as follows:

1. Slow to learn or understand; obtuse. 2. Tending to make poor decisions or careless mistakes. 3. Marked by a lack of intelligence or care; foolish or careless: 4. Dazed, stunned, or stupefied. 5. Pointless; worthless.[32]

In the Bible, "stupid" is a term used not to describe a person of low intelligence, but more for people who are capable of increasing their wisdom, but they choose not to and possess a resistance to improving themselves. As a result, biblically stupid people do make poor decisions and become foolish or careless. In the Bible, stupidity is normally accompanied by laziness and/or an inability to accept correction or knowledge.

The biblical definition of "stupid" does not involve whether a person has a high or low intelligence quotient, but much more specifically, focuses on how a person responds to the input of others. Proverbs 12:1 begins to clarify a person who is stupid in God's eyes:

Whoever loves discipline loves knowledge, but he who hates reproof is stupid.

According to God's Word, a stupid person hates to be corrected or to receive corrective discipline. A stupid person is someone who does not even understand that he does not value knowledge.

A senseless man has no knowledge, nor does a stupid man understand this. Psalm 92:6

In the workplace, when a worker has a "stupid" mentality, they simply are not receptive to correction or to the necessary information they need to properly perform a job or a task. Like the fool, that person should be quickly weeded out of the company.

Always learning and never able to come to the knowledge of the truth. 2 Timothy 3:7

---

32 - The American Heritage Dictionary of the English Language

…

Chapter 9

LIVING A BETTER LIFE
GOD'S GUIDELINES

What is the difference between information and wisdom?

How would you describe a self-serving person? Give a workplace example.

What benefits are there for seeking the advice of others before making an important financial decision?

What is God's promise to those who give to the needy?

What characteristics of the ant's work ethic can be applied to your life?

List reasons why a budget is important. If you do not have a budget, what can you do today to start one?

What does the Bible warn about being in debt?

Why does God require that you tithe?

Plan for both the predictable and the unpredictable.

Whenever I have the opportunity to share the amazing yet practical principles of Proverbs with others, individually or in conferences and seminars, one key question tends to keep popping up: "Mike, does Proverbs say anything about how I can practically live a better life today?"

As I probe the questioners further, I have learned that they are not really asking me a question so much as they are making an observation concerning their own lives; they continue to talk without waiting for an answer to their first question: "Mike, my life isn't going very well right now. We are deeply in debt, and frankly, my marriage is suffering from the financial and emotional stress. Does Proverbs suggest anything I can do to turn my life around and finally have some sort of peace? Are there any keys offered in Proverbs to practically help me lead a better life?"

My answer is always a resounding, "Absolutely!" What is amazing to me is that these questioners always seem to be astounded when I begin to explain that Proverbs provides practical guidelines concerning how to lead a better life. In this chapter, I provide a concise condensation of these practical guidelines that we all can follow to experience a better life (some of these biblical truths have also been addressed in other parts of this book, and each principle I cover here could be a book in itself). These practical guidelines from Proverbs outline how to experience a level of living where we find ourselves out of debt with a cash reserve and with a clear plan for the future, including a solid retirement income. Now that is what I call a better life!

These keys to a better life parallel the difference between information and wisdom. Information can provide you the appearance of what many would call wisdom, but information alone is not enough. "To have knowledge is to have understanding or information about something. To have wisdom is to have the ability to apply knowledge to daily life."[33] In this chapter, we will be looking at the practical principles that will help you apply knowledge to your daily life.

Charles Swindoll, in The Living Insights Study Bible, wrote: "The ultimate goal of the book of Proverbs is to take captive all the sources of knowledge and give us wisdom for living in accordance with them".[34] It is my hope that this chapter will help you take a major step towards "wisdom for living" according to God's practical principles.

1 - SEEK GOD FIRST

Trust in the Lord with all your heart and lean not on your own understanding; in all your ways submit to him, and he will make your paths straight. Proverbs 3:5-6

Leaning on our own understanding is the reason why so many people are in financial bondage today. Our own understanding is normally self-serving, but in reality our own desires and ambitions are often the wrong priorities for living a better life.

Just ask any person who has ever had a problem

---

[33] - Precept Ministries International, "The New Inductive Study Bible," page 1010, 2013, Chattanooga, TN, 37422
[34] - Swindoll, Charles, "The Living Insights Study Bible," 1996, Zondervan, Nashville, TN, 37201

with any type of addiction. Every penny they earned was spent on drugs, alcohol, sex, gambling or some other vice. The tragic story of addiction is told over and over again in Hollywood where various excesses are glorified as a desirable lifestyle, but ultimately, these addictions lead to poverty and destruction. If we cannot trust our "own understanding," then who can we trust?

Whoever gives heed to instruction prospers, and blessed is the one who trusts in the Lord. Proverbs 16:20

As we seek God first, trusting in Him and following His rules for living in His Word, we experience a better form of living with less problems, less stress, less crisis, and less chaos. And, when we do go through real trials, as we look to Him, we get through them with His grace, love and compassion.

If we seek first God, and embrace the practical principles in His Word, we will be on our way to living a better life.

2 - PREPARE A PLAN FOR LIVING AND FOLLOW IT

Proverbs soberly explains what careful planning can achieve, and it also vividly projects the catastrophic chaos that a failure to plan can ultimately produce in a person's life. Clearly, Proverbs advocates that we implement a solid plan for living, and avoid the uncertainty (no peace of mind) that little or no planning inevitably produces in our lives, and in our families or businesses.

The plans of the diligent lead to profit as surely as haste leads to poverty. Proverbs 21:5

Quick decisions, without deliberate diligence and practical planning, lead to poverty. I constantly see the ravages of quick decisions, made without any thought or planning, in my financial counseling.

For example, countless homeowners over the last few decades made hasty decisions to refinance their homes in an inflationary economy when home values (on paper) were escalating 10 to 25 percent a year. Had these same homeowners diligently looked at the history of the housing market, they would have discerned that housing prices traditionally hit peaks or bubbles, then adjust down to more honest, realistic values.

I have counseled many a homeowner that "A house is just composed of wood and drywall," and, "It is vital to think of your home as a secure place to live, not as a financial leveraging tool!" My recommendation has always been to pay off your home as soon as possible no matter what the real estate market is doing and never use your home as a vehicle to finance other purchases.

"Diligence" in Proverbs 21:5 means a "careful and methodical study of a situation before making a decision." Diligence should include consultation with others when that decision is a major one. Taking careful consideration before making serious financial decisions will protect you from most major financial mistakes.

PLAN FOR THE PREDICTABLE & THE UNPREDICTABLE

Do not boast about tomorrow, for you do not know what a day may bring. Proverbs 27:1

This particular scripture often reminds me of what is called "the volatility" of the stock market. When a stock is rising rapidly, seldom does the amateur, prospective buyer ever consider that the stock could also go down. Frankly, the stock market is very close to gambling for the average player (in the vernacular, you "play" the market; seldom is the word "investor" used when referring to stocks). This player usually makes his/her decisions based upon flimsy information such as a few words from a friend who just bought the stock. "This stock can't miss! It is going up, and it should continue to go up for some time."

My friend, only the most diligent of industry professionals, armed with comprehensive financial studies and detailed industry reports, have the available knowledge and the necessary experience of stock trends over the decades to carefully pick stocks that will, in the long range, likely prove to produce a profit (and there is still never a guarantee that the pick is a right one).

Plans are established by seeking advice; so if you wage war, obtain guidance. Proverbs 20:18

Guidance can come in many forms: a mentor, a church counselor, a successful business associate, your spouse, or a myriad of other possibilities.

Seek the advice and guidance of others before you "wage war", before you do something that will ultimately impact the status of your well-being or the status of your business.

Plans fail for lack of counsel, but with many advisers they succeed. Proverbs 15:22

In modern society, the "war" we wage could mean a new business venture, encounters with a labor union trying to tell you how to run your business, buying a larger home, or making a decision to send your child to a private or a public college. In all of these practical situations, "many advisors" can and will make a significant difference towards a desired favorable outcome.

Let the wise listen and add to their learning, and let the discerning get guidance. Proverbs 1:5

Do you see it? It is wise to listen! I cannot count the number of times someone has come to me (and then others) seeking advice on a business venture, and then, after accumulating all the wisdom of others, decided to go against the collective counsel and instead did something stupid, such as refinance their home to fund an unproven, untested new business idea.

Proverbs encourages comprehensive knowledge as a practical key to maintaining and protecting your assets:

Be sure you know the condition of your flocks, give careful attention to your herds; for riches do not endure forever, and a crown is not secure for all generations. Proverbs 27:23-24

Whatever financial transaction you are currently considering, please be sure to heed the words of Proverbs and give that transaction your "careful attention" before making a decision, knowing that things change, and that "a crown is not secure for all generations."

Knowing the condition of your flock (in modern terms, your "flock" could mean your assets, your employees, your business or your family) requires involvement: knowing the people, keeping good records, keeping track of where you are financially, and devising a plan as to where you want to be financially.

Know your employees. Intermingle with them: get to know their concerns and their problems in implementing their job assignments. In my own company I recently spent time working with each of my landscaping crews in the field, working with them openly and seeking their suggestions and recommendations for how to improve the company. I wanted to know how to help them do their jobs better.

God's wisdom tells us we need to know our financial condition because it gives us a practical picture of where we are currently. As Solomon reminded us, "riches do not endure forever!" If we are not careful in managing our money and having a careful financial plan, our assets can evaporate and not be there when we really need them.

Do not wear yourself out to get rich; do not trust your own cleverness. Proverbs 23:4

Ultimately, no matter how careful we are, Proverbs reminds us that it is the "Lord's purpose" for our lives that will prevail.

Many are the plans in a person's heart, but it is the Lord's purpose that prevails. Proverbs 19:21

3 - BE A GENEROUS GIVER

This concept has been extensively covered in Chapter Six of this book. However, it is important for me to list it again here since I am convinced from my study of Proverbs that giving is an essential, practical part of God's plan for us to live a better life. The scripture below is just one of many that has molded that conviction in me.

One person gives freely, yet gains even more; another withholds unduly, but comes to poverty. A generous person will prosper; whoever refreshes others will be refreshed. Proverbs 11:24-25

If you are gaining "even more," and if you are being "refreshed," is that not living a better life? You have already read the amazing story of Hal Taussing of Untours who gave away over 5 million dollars, and you read the testimony of his pastor concerning Hal's well-being. There are countless others like Hal who have learned this scriptural secret for living a better life. In fact, you probably know someone in your own neighborhood who is constantly giving yet seems to be the happiest guy on the block!

Part of our giving should be to the poor. God clearly has a heart for those who are struggling, and He counts on us to stand in the gap to prudently assist them (not enable them).

Whoever shuts their ears to the cry of the poor will also cry out and not be answered. Proverbs 21:13

This admonition alone should inspire all of us to give to the poor as we are able. When we "cry out" in prayer, it is always our desire that God hears and answers our needs.

It is a sin to despise one's neighbor, but blessed is the one who is kind to the needy. Proverbs 14:21

Who doesn't want to be considered blessed by God? Clearly, remembering the needy in our finances is an act that is looked upon with great favor by God.

Whoever oppresses the poor shows contempt for their Maker, but whoever is kind to the needy honors God. Proverbs 14:31

What an amazing promise; be kind to the needy and you will also be honoring God!

4 - LEARN TO BE CONTENT

This particular, practical guideline for living a

better life is one of my favorites because it speaks to the importance in a marriage for the man and wife to be able to get along without constant arguing and strife.

Better to live in a desert than with a quarrelsome and nagging wife. Proverbs 21:19

If the men reading this book mistakenly think that the wife is the main source of marriage problems according to Proverbs, that is an incorrect conclusion. The word "wife" here could just as easily be replaced with "husband." If you doubt that conclusion, just read the next two scriptures:

As charcoal to embers and as wood to fire, so is a quarrelsome person for kindling strife. Proverbs 26:21

Better a dry crust with peace and quiet than a house full of feasting, with strife. Proverbs 17:1

These scriptures clearly demonstrate that "a quarrelsome person" is the issue – and that could be the husband OR the wife. Even if your house is prospering financially and "full of feasting," that alone is not enough to live a better life. If there is "strife" there is no peace, and that strife can come from the man, the woman or even the children. In your business, the "quarrelsome person" is normally a discontented employee.

Clearly, God is saying, "You are more blessed with just a morsel of stale bread to eat in contentment than a porterhouse steak with lobster eaten in a stressful environment."

Julie and I have learned to practice this guideline in our own marriage. I remember a time when we were challenged to be content with furniture when the springs were coming out of the cushions. We had made a decision not to buy new furniture until we could pay cash for it, and that meant a time of being content with a damaged couch, for a better living experience of staying out of debt.

We drove an old jalopy that was an embarrassment to us and our children for many years, until we could buy a better car with cash. You see, these principles I am sharing with you are not just ideas I relay to others, they are practical biblical principles that my own family has practiced for decades.

Wealth alone does not make a person happy or content. You probably personally know some very wealthy people who are absolutely miserable with their lives! Wealth, by itself, is not the key to better living. However, living without strife is a major key, and frequently a lack of money to pay bills can cause strife.

Contentment is an attitude towards life, in your relationships and your finances. A person who wants to live a better life is one who learns to live at the level (within the means) that God has provided. That does not mean you do not want to improve your family situation, but it does mean that you learn to be satisfied with your current situation while you plan to improve it.

Even if you do not have that home with four bedrooms yet, learn to be content with three. In fact, many of the world's families live in one room. According to CNN Money, the average new home size in Hong Kong is 484 square feet, in the UK it is 818 square feet, and in China it is 646 square feet, while the U.S. family average is 2,164 square feet.[35]

Contentment has nothing to do with the size of your home, but it has everything to do with your attitude towards the house you live in. Ask yourself, are you praying, "Lord, thank You for the roof over our heads," or are you praying, "Lord, how long do we have to put up

---

35 - CNN Money, "How Big Is A House; Average House Size by Country," 2014, Atlanta, GA, 30303.

with this cramped place?"

STAN'S STORY OF DISCONTENTMENT

Stan became envious of his neighbor because he had a larger, more luxurious home, so Stan listed his house with a real estate firm, planning to buy something more impressive. Shortly afterwards, as Stan was reading the newspaper, he saw an ad for a house that seemed just right. Stan promptly called the realtor and said, "A house described in today's paper by your company is exactly what I'm looking for. I'd like to go see it as soon as possible!" The agent asked him several questions about the listing, then replied, "But Stan, that's your house you're describing."

Contentment is a learned attitude. Stan was learning that his attitude towards his own home needed a revision.

I always encourage others to ask this question when they are about to make an important financial decision: "Am I going to be moved to buy something that I really cannot afford, or am I going to be content with what I have now?" If you really want an item, come up with a practical plan to save for it every month until you can pay cash for it.

5 - WORK HARD

The way of the Lord is a refuge for the blameless, but it is the ruin of those who do evil. Proverbs 10:29

What is the way of the Lord? It is the principles by which He governs life. He is the king of life. He covers all things. He is the Lord of history. As the Lord, there are principles by which He rules life. If you and I learn God's ways, then we can live according to those principles and overcome strongholds. Rough times cannot shake us if we are living according to God's ways.

If we ignore God's ways or build according to our own ideas, then the rough times can and will destroy everything that was built. His principles work the same for everybody! If you violate them, you fall.

One key practical principle is to work hard. Many employees work at their jobs with very casual attitudes. They say things like, "This job is ridiculous, and my boss is an idiot!" "I'm not paid enough, so I only do just so much." "I'm only going to work when I'm being watched. If no one is paying attention, I'm not going to work at all, because if I do, then I'm an idiot!" "I will procrastinate at work and do absolutely nothing about one full day in five. That's what everybody else does."

That is the world's attitude, and it is easy to get caught up in that pessimism. However, the ant sets an example of hard work that we all can follow.

THE SAGA OF THE ANT

Go to the ant, you sluggard; consider its ways and be wise! It has no commander, no overseer or ruler, yet it stores its provisions in summer and gathers its food at harvest. Proverbs 6:6-8

The ant has no apparent boss or spouse to tell him what to do, but he still continues to work hard, storing and saving for the future. A study of the ant reveals certain characteristics that make the ant very unique, and certainly we see qualities in the ant that are worth emulating as Christians.

ANTS WORK HARD

Ants diligently look for food, look after their young, and defend the nest from unwanted visitors. Some worker ants are even given the job of taking the rubbish away from the nest and putting it outside in a special rubbish dump!

At night, the ants move the eggs and larvae deep into the nest to protect them from the cold. During the daytime, the worker ants move the eggs and larvae of the colony to the top of the nest so that they can be warmer. If a worker ant has found a good source for food, it leaves a trail of scent so that the other ants in the colony can find the food.

ANTS ARE MOTIVATED AND DISCIPLINED

The ant does not punch a timecard to be accountable to another. No one begs the ant each day to get out of bed and work. Ants are self-motivated creatures with a self-discipline that drives them each day to ensure they get their work done.

As Christians, it is important that we work whether someone is standing next to us or not. As a good worker, it is also vital to be self-starting, noticing what needs to be done in our workplace and doing it, whether we are asked to or not.

ANTS DO NOT GIVE UP

Have you ever noticed how ants always look for a way around an obstacle? You can place your finger in an ant's path and it will try to go around it or over it. It will keep looking for a way around the problem and keep going. You will never see an ant just stand and stare. It never gives up; it is always going forward.

We can all learn from the ant. There will always be obstacles in our lives, but the challenge is to keep trying, to keep going forward, to keep looking for alternative routes to get our goals accomplished. Winston Churchill probably paraphrased the ant's mindset best when he offered this priceless advice: "Never give up. Never, never give up!"

ANTS UNDERSTAND COMPOUNDING

The ant stores its provisions in the summer, careful not to consume more than it needs for the day. That is a key to financial freedom: continue to spend less than you earn.

How much food does an ant gather in the summer? All that it possibly can. Now that is a great work ethic to have. Do all you can! One ant does not worry about how much food another ant is collecting. It does not sit back and wonder why it should have to work so hard. It does not complain about the poor pay.

Success and happiness are usually the result of giving 100% – doing all you possibly can. If you look around you, you will find that successful people are those who just do all they possibly can.

ANTS SAVE WHEN THERE IS PLENTY

You need to save when you have the opportunity because when you are out of work or need money, it will be there. The ants work all summer long storing things for a time when food is not plentiful. We can do well to imitate this trait of the ant.

6 - ACCUMULATE A SAVINGS

The wise store up choice food and olive oil, but fools

gulp theirs down. Proverbs 21:20

I like this translation:

The wise man saves for the future, but the foolish man spends whatever he gets. Proverbs 21:20 TLB

We set ourselves up for failure because we do not save ahead of time for future expenses. Start to set forth a savings account for both short-term and long-term expenses.

In my consulting, I have learned that many do not like to budget, or have the will to start a budget, claiming it is "too restrictive." Yet, with budgeting and planning, the things we call "surprises" should not be surprising. For example, why should it be a surprise when a car needs new tires? The tire manufacturer supplies buyers with an estimated time of replacement for their tires. When a tire is purchased, the seller will explain, "This tire is estimated to last for approximately 40,000 miles." So where is the surprise?

Why are we surprised when we declare, "Can you believe it is Christmas already?" It seems to me that Christmas comes along at the same time each and every year. (I'm surprised that they are surprised!) Plan for the future, provide a savings for the plan, and begin to eliminate the "surprises" in your life.

7 - GET OUT OF DEBT AND STAY OUT

In 1811, over 200 years ago, Thomas Jefferson wrote a letter to his granddaughter, Cornelia Jefferson Randolph. In that letter he enclosed a list of twelve "Canons of Conduct in Life"(rules to live by). Rule Three read, "Never spend money before you have it."[36] Jefferson, as a concerned grandfather, passed on what he

---

36 - Montecello.org, "Never Spend Your Money Before You Have It," 2014, Charlottesville, VA 22902

considered one of the top ten "canons of conduct" in life. He was trying to warn his granddaughter to stay out of debt and only spend the money she had available! It has been over 200 years since his words were written, and they remain extremely valuable to this day.

THE TOP 10 FUNNY SIGNS YOU ARE BROKE

1   American Express calls and says "Please leave home without us."
2   You are formulating a plan to rob the food bank.
3   You give blood everyday...just for the free orange juice and cookie.
4   You rob Peter and then rob Paul.
5   You finally clean your house, hoping to find some loose change.
6   You think of a lottery ticket as an investment for retirement.
7   Your bologna has no first name.
8   You start washing the Styrofoam plates for reuse.
9   McDonald's supplies you with all of your kitchen condiments.
10 When you take communion, you go back for seconds.

AMERICA'S FAMILY DEBT IS GROWING DEEPER!

According to a report on CNN Money, "The rich are getting richer, and everyone else is going deeper into debt trying to keep up!"[37] The average American family is deeply in debt. They have an average credit card debt of $15,950, but the debt does not stop there. The average student loan debt is approximately $26,000, and the average household mortgage debt is about $149,700.

---

37 - CNN Money, "Debt Inequality is the New Income Inequality" money.cnn.com, May 2, 2012

Many owe more on their home than it is currently worth. The "Realty Trac" report issued in January 2014 indicated that 9.3 million properties, or 19% of all homes with mortgages, were still "deeply underwater," meaning borrowers owed at least 25% more on their mortgage than the home was worth.

Today, the average American owes approximately $47,000, while the average American salary is $41,673.84. Visa will take you any place you want to be except out of debt!

Credit card debt does not easily go away, even after death. When a family member passes away, they often leave a credit card debt behind. Many credit card companies are now sending letters to the surviving children or spouse that reads something like this:

"We have recently learned that [your mother, father, etc], a valued [name of card] customer, has passed away. Please accept our sincere apologies." The letter then offers the surviving children or the spouse the "opportunity" to assume the balance on the person's credit card with a "special introductory APR of 0% for the first six months" (the APR would increase to 13.24% after that!).[38]

Social Security furnishes the death information to the credit card companies. Unfortunately, banks are within their rights to seek payment for debts owed by a deceased borrower, and the estate is liable for the debt if it has enough money.

Did you know that the bulk of the class of 2013's debt is in government loans, with graduates owing an average of $26,000? They also hold an average of $19,000 in private loans, $18,000 in state loans, $13,000 in personal and family loans and $3,000 in credit card debt![39]

---

39 - Economy.money.ccn.com, "Americans Buried Under Debt", 2012, Atlanta, 2GA, 30303.
38 - CNN Money, "Debt After Death: Banks Chase Down Mourners," 2011, Atlanta. GA, 30303.

The rich rule over the poor, and the borrower is slave to the lender. Proverbs 22:17

When going into debt, we need to be mindful that the borrower becomes like a captive slave to the lender. A good principle is to try not to borrow and to keep financial dealings in the present as much as possible. Do not fund the present by leveraging the future. Again, in the words of Thomas Jefferson, "Never spend money before you have it."

8 - TITHE

As in all of the other guidelines I have shared in this chapter, the tithe is a topic that has already been covered to some extent in this book. The interesting thing to me about tithing is that most Christians know what tithing means and understand that it is God's desire for them to tithe so that He can release blessings into their lives.

However, the actual number of people who tithe in America is surprisingly low. The Barna Research Group has tracked tithing over a number of years, and their revelations are not encouraging. The actual percentage of adults who have been tithing has been declining over these last several years, especially in the immediate aftermath of the economic crisis in late 2008. Since that time, 2 out of 10 Americans (20%) have reduced their giving to a church or a religious center, and 31% have downsized their giving to other nonprofits.[40]

In April of 2011, Barna reported that the reductions in giving continued. The percentage of people downsizing their gifts to nonprofits rose from 31% to 39%. In this same report, they discovered that just 5% of adults tithed! 24% of evangelicals tithed, followed by 12% of conservatives, followed by people who prayed,

---

40 - Barna, George, "OmniPollSM," April, 2011, Ventura, CA, 93001, George Barna Research Group.

read the Bible and attended a church service, also at 12%, followed by charismatic or Pentecostal Christians at 11%.

Those listed as "highly unlikely to tithe" included people under the age of 25, atheists and agnostics, single adults who have never been married, liberals and downscale adults. 1% of the people in each of these segments tithed in 2011.

Only 9% of all "born-again" adults contributed one-tenth or more of their income to the church. Catholics tithed at a rate of 2%, and protestants at 8%. 17% of the adults surveyed claimed that they tithed, but only 3% actually did so. Yet, 29% of the adults surveyed actually believed the Bible commands them to tithe.[41]

I believe that the underlying reason why many people do not tithe is that they are afraid that they will not have enough money left to pay their bills. In other words, they do not believe that God will provide for them, so they fear that they will be stuck with unpaid bills.

They do not understand the principle of sowing and reaping. The unwise man has a bucket of seeds and eats all of the seeds. The wise man, even though he is hungry, just eats what he needs, then plants the seeds so that he has a harvest that will feed his family in the future and still provide seeds for the next planting.

The wise person knows that you plant seeds for a future crop. God wants to be involved in your financial future, and He wants you to live a better life. Many times in our life, Julie and I have tithed without knowing where the money to pay bills was coming from, and it was amazing how God always came through. We just kept tithing year after year and watched what He did. It is true what so many say, "You cannot out give God."

---

41 - Barna Research Group

As you practice these biblical principles, you open the door for God to bless your life and for you and your family to experience a better life according to His plan.

Chapter 10

THE FIRST AND LAST WORD

Why is getting your way by force or intimidation not a productive plan?

What is the difference between "trusting in the Lord" and making your own plans? How can you reconcile the two plans?

In what ways are you "serving love to others?"

What virtue can temper pride and arrogance? How do you develop it?

What is the real hope for America?

Anything less than the constant application of God's Word is folly.

You might say that this chapter is my last word on Proverbs. In this day and age, with radio, TV, phones, and the internet, it is getting harder and harder to share the last word on anything.

In the old days when one child would say something hurtful to another, the wronged person would retort, "Oh yeah, well sticks and stones will break my bones, but words will never hurt me." Unfortunately, that statement was wrong then, and it is wrong now.

Such was the painful lesson learned by a school administrator in Fairfax County, just outside of Washington, D.C., when he refused to call a day off from school for a snow day. One student was so upset about having to attend school in the snow that he called the administrator's home phone and, when he got the answering machine, left a blistering message.

Unfortunately, the administrator's wife heard the voice message first, became upset, and called back the student's voicemail. She kept her retort clean, but she did make it embarrassingly clear what she thought of "snot nosed little brats" bothering her at home.

Ideally, that would have been the last word,

except the student posted her entire voicemail rant on YouTube. To date, thousands have heard her message, and now they are taking sides on the issue of when to call for a snow day and debating the ethics of posting phone messages on YouTube.

In an interview with the Washington Post, the school administrator commended the student for showing the "courage of his convictions to stand up and be identified." However, wanting to have the last word, he also blamed the student for causing his wife "considerable embarrassment."

Since this entire scenario is still on the internet, my hunch is that we have not heard the final word on this debate.

In this final chapter of my book, I want to share with you some "final words" from Proverbs that will hopefully impact your life in a positive way.

FORCE AND VIOLENCE DIMINISH THE PERPETRATOR

So are the ways of everyone who gains by violence; it takes away the life of its possessors. Proverbs 1:19

In business or in your home, when you try and get your way through force, violence, or intimidation, it not only degrades your victims, it also diminishes you as the perpetrator.

Now, you might say, "I've never hit an employee," or "I don't abuse my children," and to that I say, "Great. Glad to hear it."

But, there are a number of ways to verbally hurt or abuse your employees or kill the spirit in your children through harsh words or extreme intimidation.

These rash forms of achieving "gains" in your business or home either ruin or reduce the respect you receive from others and ultimately harm even what you think about yourself ("takes away the life"), sapping your soul.

LEAN ON MORE THAN YOUR OWN UNDERSTANDING

Trust in the LORD with all your heart and do not lean on your own understanding. Proverbs 3:5

As human beings, we tend to take great pride that we can reason things out and come to a clear understanding of what to do in any situation. But Scripture warns us that simply relying on our understanding to make a decision in business, or in your family decisions, is simply not enough.

Five times in Proverbs and sixty-one times throughout God's Word, "Trust in the Lord" is repeated. Do you think it is an important point to God? Precisely, what does "Trust in the Lord" mean?

It means that we do not try to figure out everything on our own. We come to a place where we recognize that the very Creator of the universe just might have some wisdom and input for us if we will seek Him and His direction.

So that your trust may be in the LORD, I have taught you today, even you. Proverbs 22:19

Yes, "even you" can gain wisdom and understanding as you seek Him, trust Him and acknowledge Him to guide and direct your life.

In all your ways acknowledge Him, and He will make your paths straight. Proverbs 3:6

When you are seeking understanding, pray, listening for God's voice and direction for everything you do, everywhere you go, and every decision you make. God is your friend, and He is the One who will keep you on track in everything you do.

Commit your works to the LORD and your plans will be established. Proverbs 16:3

If one turns over to the Lord what he plans to do, his life purposes will come to fruition. In some cases, as we submit our plans to His, we will be convicted to put our plans aside and follow. His plan is for a greater good that we might not even fully understand until we follow and obey His direction. For example, a man might be seeking a new job. In his own plan, the job with a major company makes more earthly sense, but in his prayer time (individually and with his wife) he is being led to take the job with a smaller company. If he submits to the Lord's plan, he is likely to receive and experience unexpected benefits he could not anticipate in his own plan.

Human planning is valuable and in fact is encouraged (even mandated) by Proverbs. But, as Christians, the underlying part of all of our planning should be the recognition that the Lord God Yahweh is the ultimate and best guide for all of our plans, and we must be willing to submit all of our plans to Him, and He will direct and guide us in the best possible path. Proverbs 16:9, 20 and 33 assert that we can make all of our plans and concoct all kinds of devices to make our decisions, but ultimately, all things are in God's hands.

3 - RUN FROM EVIL; SEEK GOD'S WISDOM

Do not be wise in your own eyes; fear the LORD and turn away from evil. Proverbs 3:7

Just as it is foolishness to "lean on your own understanding," it is also foolishness to assume that somehow, someway, due to your vast reading and experiences, you now know it all. You don't!

No matter how "wise" you are in "your own eyes," you cannot survive in this world without God's direction in your life. Realize and acknowledge that whatever abilities you may have are a gift from God. Run to God and run from evil!

The fear of the LORD is to hate evil; pride and arrogance and the evil way and the perverted mouth, I hate. Proverbs 8:13

Pride and arrogance must be tempered and restricted by humility in order to keep our lives on track.

4 - GOD'S WORD MAKES YOU HEALTHY

As you apply the truths in Proverbs, *It will be healing to your body and refreshment to your bones* Proverbs 3:8. That's right. Your body will literally glow with health, and your very bones will vibrate with life!

For they are life to those who find them and health to all their body. Proverbs 4:24

Health is more than the foods you eat; it involves living as a righteous man in concert with the biblical principles in God's Word. As you do, you will have total health – inside and out.

5 - SERVE LOVE TO OTHERS

Better is a dish of vegetables where love is than a fattened ox served with hatred. Proverbs 15:17

You have probably heard stories of folks growing up in poor environments who never knew they were poor there always was laughter at the table and joy in the hearts of the family members. What they ate did not seem to matter. What you eat is not as important as how you serve it. A crust of bread shared in love is far better than a slab of prime rib served in hatred.

Better is a dry morsel and quietness with it than a house full of feasting with strife. Proverbs 17:1

6 - HOPE FOR OUR NATION

By the transgression of a land many are its princes, but by a man of understanding and knowledge, so it endures. Proverbs 28:2

As I read this final passage I share here from Proverbs, I think to myself, "There is hope for America." You see, that hope is in the Christian leaders God raises up with biblical "understanding and knowledge" to fix whatever situations need to be fixed through the application of biblical principles.

It seems that everyone who can get near a microphone has "a plan" to fix what is wrong with our economy and our country. But, unless their ideas line up with biblical principles, the chances of success are minimal.

After reading this book, hopefully you now understand that only men and women with deep biblical wisdom and understanding can successfully lead our country, lead a business, or manage a family. Anything less than the constant application of God's Word is folly.

The next time you hear one of our leaders declaring that they have the way out, examine their remarks by applying this simple biblical observation:

By the blessing of the upright a city is exalted, but by the mouth of the wicked it is torn down. Proverbs 11:11

Are you leading others by living a biblically upright life? Perhaps the best way I can recommend to help you evaluate the answer to that question is by reading Romans 12. This passage is perhaps the best summary of the Book of Proverbs that I know, and serves as the final Word for all of us on this road to becoming more like Him.

Therefore I urge you, brethren, by the mercies of God, to present your bodies a living and holy sacrifice, acceptable to God, which is your spiritual service of worship. And do not be conformed to this world, but be transformed by the renewing of your mind, so that you may prove what the will of God is, that which is good and acceptable and perfect.

For through the grace given to me I say to everyone among you not to think more highly of himself than he ought to think; but to think so as to have sound judgment, as God has allotted to each a measure of faith. For just as we have many members in one body and all the members do not have the same function, so we, who are many, are one body in Christ, and individually members one of another. Since we have gifts that differ according to the grace given to us, each of us is to exercise them accordingly: if prophecy, according to the proportion of his faith; if service, in his serving; or he who teaches, in his teaching; or he who exhorts, in his exhortation; he who gives, with liberality; he who leads, with diligence; he who shows mercy, with cheerfulness.

Let love be without hypocrisy. Abhor what is evil; cling to what is good. Be devoted to one another in brotherly love; give preference to one another in honor; not lagging behind in diligence, fervent in spirit, serving the Lord; rejoicing in hope, persevering in tribulation, devoted to prayer, contributing to the needs of the saints, practicing hospitality. Bless those who persecute you; bless and do not curse. Rejoice with those who rejoice, and weep with those who weep. Be of the same mind toward one another; do not be haughty in mind, but associate with the lowly. Do not be wise in your own estimation. Never pay back evil for evil to anyone. Respect what is right in the sight of all men. If possible, so far as it depends on you, be at peace with all men. Never take your own revenge, beloved, but leave room for the wrath of God, for it is written, "Vengeance is Mine, I will repay," says the Lord. "But if your enemy is hungry, feed him, and if he is thirsty, give him a drink; for in so doing you will heap burning coals on his head." Do not be overcome by evil, but overcome evil with good.

Other books by Mike LaBahn:

Giving God's Way
Radical Generosity Will Change Your Life.

Our Giving Story
Some Aspire to Make a Million.
We Aspired to Give A Million.

Get Free
A Short Guide to Financial Well-Being from The Wisdom of Proverbs.

Available at **mikelabahn.com**

10 - THE FIRST AND LAST WORD / 179